TALES FROM THE HALFDECK

The Apprentice Midshipman's logbook for Blue Funnel Line

James B Wood
Captain Philip J Wood

Perwood Publications

Copyright © 2023 James B Wood & Philip J Wood

The authors assert the moral right to be identified as the author of this work.

All rights reserved. No part of this book may be used or reproduced by any means, graphic, electronic, or mechanical, including photocopying, recording, taping, or by any information storage retrieval system without the written permission of the publisher except in the case of brief quotations embodied in critical articles and reviews.

Cover design by Victoria Mooring

Perwood Publications
www.woodclan.co.uk

For Oskar, Embla, Charlotte, Cici, Matthew, Jackson and Emily

CONTENTS

Title Page	
Copyright	
Dedication	
Foreword from the authors	1
List of Ships & Vessels Mentioned	5
Glossary of Nautical Terms, Acronyms & Slang	11
M.V. Glenroy	15
S.S. Ulysses	33
M.V. Ajax	60
M.V. Glenearn	73
M.V. Glengyle	83
M.V. Glenogle	89
M.V. Clytoneus	122
M.V. Automedon	154
S.S. Hector	184
After the Halfdeck	207
Ships Served & Ranks	212
Footnotes – Vessel reference	215
Acknowledgement	221
Books By This Author	223

FOREWORD FROM THE AUTHORS

When I was younger I was regaled with stories of going round the world in the Merchant Navy. Getting suits made in Hong Kong, visiting Brisbane over Christmas before it was a sprawling city and Phuket's Buckets – which is far more amusing if you are pronouncing the "Ph" as "F".

Having wanted to go to sea since the age of ten, when my father's brother, David, joined as an apprentice with the BP Tanker company, as it sounded like a bit of fun and for a boy born during the war, anything was more fun than the bombed-out streets of London – although the stories of playing in the bomb craters while avoiding getting tetanus from rusty nails have their own charm.

Having therefore decided that a life at sea was the future and being informed by a reputable source (a fellow apprentice of David's who was an old boy of the London Nautical School) that by attending LNS for pre-sea training would reduce the apprenticeship to three and half years, mid-year P. J. Wood transferred from Wimbledon Grammer School to the London Nautical School. Joining for the last term of year 3 and after one term in year 4, he had to jump a whole school year to the 5th year and complete the last 2 terms for his GCEs because LNS and the school master's had told him he would be too old for an apprenticeship had he not jumped that year.

Attaining his GCEs in Navigation, Seamanship, English, Maths and General Science. Captain Harvey, the deputy head at the time, suggested that Blue Funnel had a good reputation for apprenticeships and that he should apply there.

The Apprentice's Indenture that he and his father signed in October of 1961 binding him to the company for the next 3 ½ years seems a little quaint nowadays.

This book is meant to give you an insight into the life and times of a 16-year-old and growing up in a world lost to merchant mariners of today, but not forgotten by those who sailed on the many ships of the Blue Funnel Line and Glen Line [known as Ocean Trading & Transport Company since 1972] and the other shipping companies involved in movement of goods across the world.

Kids have it easy these days, in education until they are 18, entertainment and computers everywhere, health and safety stopping them from being endangered in any meaningful way. In the 1960's it was different - Philip left for a life at sea as an apprentice midshipman when he was 16 years old, just seven days before his 17th birthday.

Join us on a journey at sea between 1961 and 1965 when the British merchant ship companies really did rule the waves. Sailing on liner/cargo ships between the UK, Far East and Australia.

With seven grandchildren with ages ranging from 3 to 18, we thought this book would be an important historical document for them to read about how, my father, their Grandpa, went round the world, through the Panama Canal, Suez Canal, across the international date line and over the equator on ships in the early 1960's. Learning about the day-to-day things he had to contend with, and giving some context to his many stories and wonder why he went shopping so much, as he hates it so much now.

For example – it is mentioned 31 times that he went "shopping", however only 4 items (Binoculars x2, Radio and an electric toy) were ever mentioned being purchased... this was an euphemism for drinking as it was made very clear in the Indenture it was forbidden for an apprentice to frequent Taverns or Alehouses.

The names of cities, ports and countries have been left as they were written in the 1960's, this is not to insult or offend the people of those places whose names may have changed but we feel this is a historic record and should reflect the time of writing.

As a note - any phrases or words within ( ) were written at the time by P. J. Wood and any phrases or words within [ ] were added by myself whilst I was transcribing the document.

Finally, I corrected major errors of grammar for clarity, but left it mostly as written which would explain the multiple ways of spelling certain words which you can marvel at in the Glossary of Nautical Terms, Acronyms & Slang.

– *Apprentice's Indenture* –

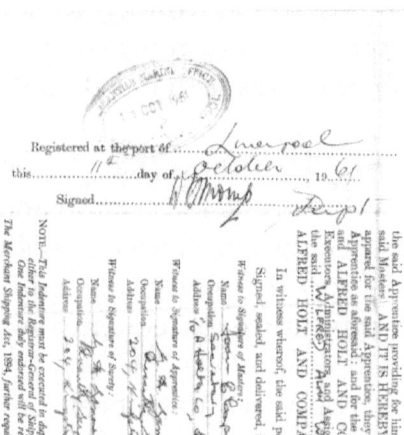

APPRENTICE'S INDENTURE.

Registered at the port of ...Liverpool...
this ...11th... day of ...October... 19 61
Signed ....

This Indenture, made the 9th day of October, 19 61, Between ...Philip John Wood..., born the 1st ..., in ...Cheltenham..., in the county of ...Gloucester..., now residing at ...104 Kingston Road, Staines, Middx.... of the one part, ALFRED HOLT AND COMPANY, of Liverpool, of ...India Buildings, Water Street, Liverpool 2... and ...Alan Wood Esq, Surrey... of the second part, and ...Alan Wood... ...of Sunbury... of the third part.

WITNESSETH That the said ...Philip John Wood... hereby voluntarily binds himself Apprentice unto the said ALFRED HOLT AND COMPANY, and their Assigns, for the term of 3 YRS 6 MOS years from the date hereof; And the said Apprentice hereby covenants that, during such time, the said Apprentice will faithfully serve his said Masters, and their Assigns, and obey their lawful commands, and keep their secrets, and will, when required, give to them true accounts of their goods and money which may be committed to his charge, or come into the hands, of the said Apprentice; and that the said Apprentice will not, during the said term, do any damage to his said Masters, or their Assigns, nor will he consent to any such damage being done by others, but will, if possible, prevent the same, and give warning thereof; and will not embezzle or waste the Goods of his said Masters, or their Assigns, nor give or lend the same to others without their licence; nor absent himself from their service without leave; nor frequent Taverns or Alehouses, unless upon their business; nor play at unlawful games. IN CONSIDERATION WHEREOF, the said Masters hereby covenant with the said Apprentice, that during the said term they, the said Masters, and their Assigns, will and shall use all proper means to teach the said Apprentice or cause him to be taught the business of a Seaman, and so long as he applies himself diligently thereto, of a ship's officer."

and the said Apprentice also agrees to provide for himself all wearing apparel and necessaries (except such as are herein before specially agreed to be provided by the said Masters; AND IT IS HEREBY AGREED, that if at any time during the said term, the said Masters, or their Assigns, provide any the necessary Apparel for the said Apprentice, they may deduct any sums properly expended thereon, by them, from the sums so agreed to be paid to the said Apprentice as aforesaid; and for the performance of the agreements herein contained, each of them, the said ...Philip John Wood... and ALFRED HOLT AND COMPANY, doth hereby bind himself, his Heirs, Executors, and Administrators, unto the other of them, their Executors, ...Whippingham... and Assigns, in Honour; and for the performance of the covenants on the part of the said Apprentice herein contained, the said ALFRED HOLT AND COMPANY, and their Assigns, in Honour.

Medical and Surgical Assistance, and to pay to the said Apprentice the sum of £ ...v.v..v........, in the manner following: (that is to say),

£ 90 : : : for the first six months,
£206 : : : for the first year afterwards,
£268 : : : for the second year,
£350 : : : for the third and final year.

In witness whereof, the said parties have hereunto set their hands and seals, the day and year above written.

Signed, sealed, and delivered, in the presence of

Witness to Signature of Masters:
Name ....
Occupation ......
Address ....

.... (Master)

Witness to Signature of Apprentice:
Name ....
Occupation ....
Address ....

.... (Apprentice)

Witness to Signature of Surety:
Name ....
Occupation ....
Address ....

.... (Surety)

NOTE.— This Indenture must be executed in duplicate, and one portion to whom the Apprentice is bound must, within seven days of the execution of the Indenture, take or transmit either to the Registrar-General of Shipping and Seamen, Tower Hill, London, E.C.3, or to the Superintendent of a Mercantile Marine Office, both Indentures to be recorded. One Indenture duly endorsed will be returned to the Masters of the Apprentice.

The Merchant Shipping Act, 1894, further requires the Masters to notify, any assignment or cancellation of Indentures, or the death or desertion of the Apprentice.

LIST OF SHIPS & VESSELS MENTIONED

Agapenor – Built in 1947 – DWT: 7,664 – In 1967 she had to be abandoned to insurers after becoming trapped by closure of Suez Canal. In 1975 she became Panamanian registered and renamed Nikos.

Ajax – Built in 1958 – DWT: 7,969 – In 1972 renamed Deucalion and in 1973 sold to Macao renamed Kailock.

Anchises – Built in 1946 – DWT: 7,642 – In 1973 she was renamed Alcinous and was scrapped in 1975.

Antilochus – Built in 1949 – DWT: 7,635 – In 1977 she was sold to Gulf (Shipowners) Ltd, London and renamed Gulf Orient.

Arcadia – Launched in 1953 – Owned and operated by P&O. During the 1960's she did a mixture of line voyage interspersed with cruises from Britain and Australia, including trans-Pacific routes. She was scrapped in 1979.

Ascanius – Built in 1950 – DWT: 7,692 – In 1972 she was transferred to Elder Dempster Line and renamed Akosombo, in 1973 she reverted to Ascanius and in 1976 sold to Saudi-Europe Line where she was renamed Mastura.

Atreus – Built in 1951 – DWT: 7,800 – In 1977 she was sold to Sherwood Shipping Company, Singapore and renamed United Valiant.

Autolycus – Built in 1949 – DWT: 7,635 – In 1976 she was sold to Gulf (Shipowners) Ltd based in London and renamed Gulf Trader.

Bar Lightvessel – Mersey Bar [53°32'1"N 3°20'59"W] From 1960 to 1972 the vessel was stationed on Bar Station, Liverpool

Bay. Since 2006 she has been used as a cafe, bar and museum in Canning Dock.

Battleship Texas (BB-35) – Launched in 1912 and decommissioned in 1948. The Battleship Texas was the first U.S. permanent battleship Museum.

Benavon – Built in 1949 – DWT: 7,845 – in 1970 sold to Panama and renamed Liziana.

Bendoran – Built in 1956 – DWT: 10,142 – Completed for Ben Line Steamers Ltd. - Wm. Thomson & Co., Leith. In 1977 she was scrapped.

Bengloe – Built in 1961 – DWT: 11,282 - Scrapped in 1978.

Breckonshire – Built in 1940 – DWT: 9,061 – In 1941 requisitioned and renamed Empire Activity. In 1942 she became HMS Activity. In 1946 she was returned to Glen Line and renamed Breckonshire. Scrapped in 1967.

Canberra – Launched in 1960 – Operated originally under the combined P&O–Orient Line service between the United Kingdom and Australasia. After service in the Falklands war [1982], she continued as a cruise liner under various owners and operators until her last voyage in October 1997 and sold for scrap.

Cathay – Built in 1957 – DWT: 13,351 – In 1961 P&O purchased from CMB, Antwerp and renamed Cathay, in 1976 she was sold to China and renamed Kenghsin.

Clytoneus – Built in 1948 – DWT: 7,620 – Scrapped in 1972.

Diomed – Built in 1956 – DWT: 7,980 – In 1970 she was transferred to Glen Line and renamed Glenbeg. In 1972 she reverted to Diomed and in 1973 was sold to Macao and renamed Kaising.

Doctor Lykes – Built 1945 – DWT: 7,854 - Standard ship type C3-S-BH1 built for United States Maritime Commission, she was scrapped in 1973.

ELBE 3 Lightvessel – Built in 1888 as the Weser lightship. Since 1979 it now moored at the Övelgoenne museum harbour in Hamburg-Neumühlen

Elbe I Lightvessel (Lightship ELBE 1) – Launched in 1943, it did not go into service until 1948. While in operation it was considered the largest lightship in the world. Operations were stopped in 1988 and it is now a Maritime Museum located in Cuxhaven, Germany.

Ellinis – Launched in 1932 – Originally owned by Matson Lines, she was bought by Chandris Lines in 1963 and ran a regular service between England, Greece and Australia. She was scrapped in 1987.

English Star – Built in 1950 – DWT: 9,996 – Owned by Blue Star Line Ltd and she was sold to Chin Tai Enterprise Co. Ltd., Taiwan in 1973 and scrapped.

Eumaeus – Built in 1953 – DWT: 7,681 – In 1962 she was transferred to NSMO (Dutch) and in 1978 scrapped.

Fleetbank – Built in 1953 – DWT: 5,690 – In 1970 she was sold to Lalis & Boudros, Greece and renamed Lady Ute.

Flintshire – Built in 1962 – DWT: 11,926 – In 1978 sold to Liberia and renamed Orient Express.

Glenartney – Built in 1940 – DWT: 9,795 – Scrapped in 1967.

Glenfinlas – Built in 1946 – DWT: 7,639 – Completed as Calchas for China Mutual Steam Navigation Company (Taken over by Alfred Holt & Co. in 1902) In 1957 she was chartered to Glen Line and renamed Glenfinlas, in 1962 reverted to Calchas and in 1973 scrapped after fire at Kelang, Malaysia.

Glenogle – Built in1962 – DWT: 11,918 – In 1978 she was sold to Hong Kong and renamed Harvest.

Glenroy – Built in 1938 – DWT: 9,809 – Scrapped in 1966.

Gorgon – Built in 1933 – DWT: 3,533 – A joint Blue Funnel and West Australia company, she was scrapped in 1964.

Hector – Built in 1949 – DWT: 10,125 – Scrapped in 1972.

Helenus – Built in 1949 – DWT: 10,125 – Scrapped in 1978.

Himalaya – Launched in 1948 – DWT: 9,659 – S.S. Himalaya was P&O and operated mainly between United Kingdom and Australia. She was withdrawn from service in 1974 and scrapped the next year.

HMS Lion – Commissioned in 1960 – DWT: 12,080 – Having been rushed into service with some shortcuts in the engineering department, due to political pressure to get her to sea, but she was not fully operational until 1961. She reached East Asia in early 1963. She was present at the Malaya independence celebrations in 1963 and the Maltese independence celebrations in 1964 before being decommissioned in 1972.

HMS Albion – Commissioned in 1954 – DWT: 24,000 – Originally joining the Mediterranean fleet, she was part of the Suez crisis. In 1961 conversion begun to a commando carrier and she recommissioned in 1962 before joining the Far East Fleet. She had the nickname of "The Old Grey Ghost of the Borneo Coast" – She was scrapped in 1973.

Ixion – Built in 1951 – DWT: 10,125 – Scrapped in 1972.

Jason – Built in 1950 – DWT: 10,125 – Scrapped in 1972.

Laomedon – Built in 1953 – DWT: 7684 – In 1977 she was sold to Panama and renamed Aspasia.

Memnon – Built in 1959 – DWT: 8,504 – In 1975 she was renamed Stentor and in 1977 transferred to Elder Dempster Line and renamed Owerri. In 1978 she was sold to Greece and renamed Europe.

Menelaus – Built in 1957 – DWT: 8,538 - In 1972 transferred to Elder Dempster Line, renamed Mano, in 1977 renamed Oti and in 1978 sold to Greece and renamed Elstar.

Menestheus – Built in 1958 – DWT: 8,510 – In 1977 she was transferred to Elder Dempster Line and renamed Onitsha. In 1978 she was sold to Cyprus and renamed Elisland.

Oranje – Built in 1938 – DWT: 20,565 – Owned by Nederland Line, laid up and used as a hospital ship during the war, she was sold to Lauro Line, Italy in 1964, she was renamed Angelina Lauro.

Orcades – Built in 1948 – DWT: 28,472 – Originally built for the Orient Line, in 1962 transferred to P&O Line ownership and in 1973 she was scrapped.

Orestes – Built in 1924 – DWT: 7,845 – Scrapped in 1963.

Oronsay – Built in 1951 – DWT: 28,136 – Originally built for the Orient Line, in 1962 she was transferred to P&O Line and in 1975 she was scrapped.

Perseus – Built in 1950 – DWT: 10,109 – Scrapped in 1973.

Polydorus – Built in 1945 – DWT: 7,671 – ex- Salina Victory, in 1946 purchased from US Maritime Commission, renamed Polydorus, operated by NSOM (Dutch), 1960 transferred to Blue Funnel, renamed Talthybius during the 1960's, in 1971 she was scrapped.

Pyrrhus – Built in 1949 – DWT: 10,093 – Scrapped in 1972.

Rhexenor – Built in 1945 – DWT: 10,199 – Scrapped in 1975.

Royal Sovereign Lt. ship – Royal Sovereign shoals [50°43'24"N 0°26'08"E]. A sandbank 6.8 miles offshore of Eastbourne. The lightvessel was replaced with Royal Sovereign lighthouse 1971.

S. Goodwin Lt. Ship – Goodwin Sands [51°13'18"N 1°36'21"E]. LV69 was sunk on station by a mine in October 1940. The replacement, LV90, sank on 27 November 1954 when cables to her two sea anchors broke in a hurricane-force storm. With the loss of seven souls. The next replacement ship was decommissioned on 26 July 2006.

Soudan – Built in 1947 – DWT: 9,080 – Part of the P&O fleet, Scrapped in 1970.

Stentor – Built in 1946 – DWT: 10,203 – In 1958 transferred to Glen Line and renamed Glenshiel. In 1963 she reverted to Stentor and in 1975 was scrapped.

Stratheden – Built in 1937 – DWT: 23,732 – Built for the P&O Line. She was sold in 1964 to John Latsis, Piraeus, and renamed Henrietta Latsis.

Sunk Lightvessel – Sunk Sands [51°49'35"N 1°30'40"E]. Stationed in the Thames Estuary since 1802. It was replaced in 2007 by Sunk Centre as part of a new Traffic Separation Scheme.

Tantalus – Built in 1945 – DWT: 7,674 – Originally known as Polyphemus an ex- Macmurray Victory ship, in 1946 it was purchased from US Maritime Commission and renamed, operated by NSOM (Dutch), in 1960 transferred to Blue Funnel and renamed Tantalus, in 1969 sold to Greece renamed Pelops and scrapped.

Tjiwangi – Built in 1950 – DWT: 6,264 – Originally owned and operated by Royal Interocean Lines, she was sold to Pacific

International Lines in 1971 and renamed Kota Bali. She was scrapped in 1980.

Tongue lightship – Tongue Sands [51°30′39″N 1°23′5″E]. Stationed in the North Sea, 8 miles north of Margate.

Ulysses – Built in 1949 – DWT: 8,976 – In 1971 sold to Cyprus and renamed Aegis Saga

Ships mentioned within the log which we could not find the history of, or at least a history that was available to research online:

Lucia
Aberdean
Naya
William Rays

GLOSSARY OF NAUTICAL TERMS, ACRONYMS & SLANG

A.B. – Able Seaman.

A.P. – Aft Peak.

Aldis battery – A battery for a signal lamp or Aldis Lamp (see below)

Aldis Lamp - A signal lamp (also called a Morse lamp) is a signalling device that uses flashes of light using Morse code.

Barbarising – Cleaning a wooden deck.

Binnacle – A waist-high case that houses a ship's compass, mounted in front of the helmsman.

Bluey – Affectionate term for Blue Funnel Line ships.

B.T. – Ballast Tank.

Bulwarks – the Extension of a ship's sides above the level of the deck.

Chippy, Chippies – Slang term for a Carpenter.

Coaming – A raised section of deck plating around a hatch.

Cwt(s) – Abbreviation for hundred weight, also known as centum weight.

Davit – A crane used for supporting, raising, and lowering a lifeboat.

D.B. – Double Bottom

Deck Quoits – A maritime version of the game Quoits where the quoits are invariably made of rope, to avoid damaging the ship's deck.

Deck Cricket Balls – As the crew kept losing balls over the side of the ship, they would not pay for actual cricket balls, so the crew used rope to make monkey's fist knots to use.

Derrick – A crane/lifting device for moving cargo on a ship.

D.F. or D.F Bearings – Radio direction finding – the use of radio transmissions to find a position line of the ship.

Dhobi – Washing clothes and also an Indian term for washerman.

Dhobying – British naval term for the washing of clothes; laundry.

Dodger – A spray hood, it is an enclosed structure that protects you from waves, wind and weather.

Dog – A term for a lever that is used to secure closed a watertight door or hatch. To dog the doors means to close the doors and secure them in a closed position.

Dog Watch, Dog Watches – A watch that no one wants to work, normally the evening watch 6-8.

D.R. – Dead Reconning.

D.T. – Deep Tank

Dunnage – Packaging material used to prevent any damage to the goods in the locker or ship's hold. It helps keep the containers/cargo in place during transportation. Normally wooden blocks, boards, burlaps, and paper are used for such purposes.

E.D.(s) – Ships clerks.

Fiddley, Fiddely, Fidley, Fiddly – An iron framework around a ladder of a hatch in a ship's deck leading below the deck. Or an alleyway across decks and roofed usually with a grating for ventilation.

Focs'le, Fo'c'sle, Focsle – the forward part of the upper deck of a ship.

For'ard, For'd - Used to represent a nautical pronunciation of forward.

F.S.A. – Full Steam Away.

F.W.E. – Finished With Engines.

Halfdeck – Generally housed the Midshipman's

accommodation, the portion of a ship below the spar deck between mainmast and cabin.

Halyard, Halliard - A line or rope used to hoist a sail or flag, halyards can also be used to support other equipment on a ship, such as an anchor or a yardarm.

Holy Stone, Holystone – A large, flat piece of sandstone used for scouring a ship's wooden deck. A block of soft sandstone used for scrubbing the wooden decks of a ship, usually with sand and seawater.

Lecky – Slang term for an Electrician.

L.G. – Let Go.

L.H. – Lower Hold.

Lighters – Barges towed by tugs to larger ships to discharge or load cargo.

Lightship, Lightvessel, Lt. – The first lightship was the Nore lightship (a sandbank at the mouth of the Thames) which started operations in 1734. A lightvessel is a named for position the vessel is placed, rather than the ship. These vessels can be transferred between different stations during their lifetime.

L.T.D. – Lower Tween Deck.

M.A.R. – Mid Apprenticeship Release course.

Middy, Middys, Middies – Slang term for a Midshipmen apprentice.

The Missions to Seamen – (Now known as The Mission to Seafarers) a Christian charity serving merchant crews around the world. It operates through a global Mission 'family' network of chaplains, staff and volunteers. [https://www.missiontoseafarers.org/]

Mules – Electric trains that are a safety feature for ships to be guided through the lock chambers of the Panama Canal, also known as mulas.

O.D. – Orlop Deck (see below)

Orlop Deck – The platform over the hold of a ship that makes up the lowest deck. It is where cables are stowed, usually below the water line.

Ovies – Overalls.

Peggies – Junior midshipmen, responsible for cleaning the halfdeck, making the tea etc.

P.O.B. – Pilot on Board.

Red Lead – An anti-corrosive primer coating over exterior steelwork generally used on the hull and above-water line steel.

R.T. – Radio Telephone.

S.B.E. – Stand by Engines.

Scuppers – Drain holes on the Deck, toe rail or in bulwarks to allow water to drain overboard.

Smoko – Slang term for a smoke break or tea break.

Soogied, Soogieing, Soogie, Soogi, Sugied, Sugyed, Syging, Soogee – A type of strong cleaning product for wood and paint on board a ship. To wash with strong cleaning product.

S.O.S. – Senior Ordinary Seaman – to be honest, we couldn't work out what this abbreviation meant in relation to the text and used our best guess.

Spark, Sparkie – Electrician.

Stockholm Tar – A thick liquid used to preserve natural rope and timber. Traditionally used to coat servings on rigging and is the substance added to oakum to stop it rotting.

T.D. – Tween Deck, located between the main deck and the upper deck of a ship.

U.T.D. – Upper Tween Deck.

Wharfies – Slang term for a dock workers or stevedores.

M.V. GLENROY

November 1961

Master: D. Stewart
Mate: J. Willows
2nd Mate: A. Minshall
3rd Mate: T. Dick
4th Mate: J. Inglis

<u>Midshipmen</u>
- J. Cummings
- P.J. Delaney
- T. Williamson
- P.J. Wood

"At the outset of any great venture it is well to have your objectives clearly in mind. To be an officer and ultimately a Master in our service will demand qualities of character and ability that can only be developed through the years, but your apprenticeship, if properly used, will give you your greatest single opportunity to succeed."

- *Midshipman Appointment Letter from Alfred Holt & Co. circa 1960*

Voyage of M.V. Glenroy - Map

Voyage Statistics

Tuesday 7th November 1961 - Departure [London]

Wednesday 17th November 1961 - Port Said

Suez Canal Transit

Tuesday 21st November 1961 - Port of Aden

Thursday 30th November 1961 - Penang

Sunday 3rd December 1961 - Singapore

Wednesday 6th December 1961 - Port Swettenham (Port Klang)

Sunday 10th December 1961 - Port Dickson

Saturday 16th December 1961- Holt's Wharf (Hong Kong)

Friday 22nd December 1961 - Yokohama

Sunday 24th December 1961 - Shimizu

Monday 25th December 1961 - Kobe

Saturday 30th December 1961 - Tsingtao

Wednesday 3rd January 1962 - Hong Kong

Total number of Ports visited: 13
Total Voyage time: 58 days
Total Voyage Distance*: 14,277 Nautical miles

* All distances are estimated using Reed's New Maritime Distance Tables (1965) [Acquired from Fenton Steamship Co. Chartering and S&P department] and by going "old school" with Lloyds Atlas of World Shipping Ports (30th Edition). Ports, wharfs, jetties and buoys have all changed dramatically over

the last 62 years so that calculating accurate distances is nearly impossible to determine, so we used our best judgement.

Friday 3rd November 1961.
London
We arrived at the ship at about 1900 hours and unpacked. At 2000 hours John, Tony and I went up to London and returned about midnight.

Saturday 4th November 1961.
Breakfast at 0700 hours after which we collected our blankets and curtains. The halfdeck is far better now that the curtains are up. John and I had permission from the Mate to go home. We left at 1000 hours.

Sunday 5th November 1961.
I returned to the ship at about 2200 hours and turned in about 2300 hours.

Monday 6th November 1961.
After breakfast we cleaned the halfdeck in readiness for the pre sailing inspection by the marine superintendents. After the inspection we signed on and sent off our allotment notes. During the afternoon we are told that we are not sailing tonight and in the atmosphere of anti-climax actual home sickness settles on me. Tony and I went ashore about 1900 hours, and we returned about 2300 hours.

Tuesday 7th November 1961.
Until lunchtime our job is to mainly clean the halfdeck. After lunch, I went ashore to do some shopping. I returned in time for dinner, after which preparations for sailing were undertaken. At 2100 hours I helped the 4th Mate to clear the propellers of barges. At 2200 we sailed, and my job was on the gangway. When this was completed, the quartermaster and I stood by with the pilot ladder. When we were in the lock for the first river Pilot came aboard. At 0030 I was turned out to help with the pilot ladder to pick up the Second River Pilot, I turned in at 0100.

Wednesday 8th November 1961.
I was on day work and in the morning, I scrubbed out the

halfdeck and generally cleaned the place up. After lunch the Mate let me get on with some office work as the weather was not favourable for deck work. The sea was 'rough' for most of the day.

Thursday 9th November 1961.
Again, I was unable to do any work on the deck, so I cleaned the halfdeck and did some more office work. The sea was 'moderate'.

Friday 10th November 1961.
Tony was on day work as well today and we cleaned two lockers on port boat deck and two on the starboard boat deck. I then went round checking the lifebuoy lights with Third Mate. The sea was 'slight swell'.

Saturday 11th November 1961.
After cleaning up the halfdeck, Tony and I reported to the Second Mate on the bridge for some work. We cleaned out the two lockers in the chartroom and the three bridge lockers. We had the afternoon off. In the evening the weather took a turn for the worse and the wind picked up. We reduced speed, altered course and finally headed West back for Gibraltar.

Sunday 12th November 1961.
We had today off. After breakfast I did some reading and then change the Linen and picked up some more stores, from then until lunch I read. After lunch I repaired my razor case. We altered course this morning at 0520. The weather seems to be improving and is good at the moment. The clocks went back half an hour tonight.

Monday 13th November 1961.
Ginger joined Tony and I on the day work. We had to prepare the bulkheads and deckheads for painting. In the afternoon we began painting some of the fleets in the deckhead. At 1700 Tony and I had our second Polio "jabs".

Tuesday 14th November 1961.

Today started at 0630 and we began by cleaning the halfdeck. After breakfast Tony and I helped the electrician's collect the fan filters, whilst Ginge carried on painting the halfdeck on his own. When all the filters were collected we began to clean them in Paraffin. This took until after lunch, when the filters were washed and dried, they were soaked in oil and replaced.

Wednesday 15th November 1961.

All three of us on day work finished off the white painting in the living quarters of the halfdeck. There weren't many ships, and the sea was calm.

Thursday 16th November 1961.

We started the white painting in the bathroom and lavatory, and I spent a frustrating morning painting around the pipes and ports. We had the afternoon off when I wrote 5 letters to be posted at Port Said. There is just the black to be done in the halfdeck now, but this cannot be started until the mooring ropes are taken off the store of black paint. We turned in early as we had to get up early in the morning and we had a late-night last night because the Third Mate was educating us on radar, stars, ships and Alfred Holt and Co.

Friday 17th November 1961.

I was called at 0145 to go to on engine room stand-by for entering Port Said. The heat in the engine room seemed very intense at first, but after a cup of tea I felt quite comfortable. Nothing happened until 0245 approx. and then time flew past until 0335, when the double ring of the engine Room, telegraphs announced finished with engines. When I reached the deck, I was cool, and I had a look around the harbour. The point that struck me the most was the number of small boats powered by steam engines, and every now and again letting out a little shrill whistle.

I turned in about 0400, feeling happy at the thought of mail. I had not been in bed more than three minutes when Ginge came in with our mail. Not a single letter for me. At first, I was annoyed at my friends, but then I realised that the only people who had letters were the people whose letters came straight to the Port Said agents. All my letters were to have been forwarded by the Correspondence department. This shows a large breach in efficiency, and one that leads to despondency among the receivers of mail especially me.

I turned to at, 0600, and went to relieve Tony down on #5 hatch. At first, I was dead scared, but by the time they had finished at 0710, I felt far more confident. After breakfast, I relieved Ginge on the bridge while he went for his breakfast. We actually started down the canal at about 0830. From 0900 I had to finish off the halfdeck by painting all the black. I finish this by about 1500 and by this time we were moved in the cut to wait the northbound convoy, Tony and I went for a swim. We left the cut at about 1900 and I was on stand-by aft with the Second Mate. After this I was free.

Saturday 18th November 1961.
Ginge and I turned to after breakfast and took all the gear out of #3 lifeboat ready for tarring. Tony and I went swimming in the pool, which had just been rigged on the forward well deck.

Sunday 19th November 1961.
We had Sunday off. in the morning. I worked out an error and in the afternoon, I had an hour on the wheel. Tony and I went swimming. The weather was fine.

Monday 20th November 1961.
We turned to at 0530 and I cleaned the room out. Afterwards, Tony and I checked the stores in the lifeboats with the Third Mate.

Tuesday 21st November 1961.
We turned to at 0530 and all worked in the halfdeck. Just before breakfast we went to stand-by in readiness for entering Aden. I was on the pilot ladder after breakfast. John, Tony, and I went ashore. I went straight to Khormaksar [Now known Aden

International Airport] to try and see my uncle [Uncle Parky – MOD man who was a close personal friend of my Father and worked with him at Sperry's during the war]. After a lot of trouble, I found out that he would not be back until lunchtime. When he eventually arrived, we had lunch together. He then showed me around the town, and we reached the pier at by 1445 so that I could be back by 1500. Captain Stuart was waiting on the pier as well, so I returned to the ship with him and I was aboard at 1515, mainly because the agents' boat didn't get to the pier until 1511. For leaving Aden I was on the poop stand by.

Wednesday 22nd November 1961.
Turned to at 0530 and we continued to paint the lifeboats. I spent most of the day painting "mast colours" in the boat and on the bottom boards.

Thursday 23rd November 1961.
Turn to at 0530 and started to put the boat back, it was like a "3-D" jigsaw puzzle without a plan. About 1000 Tony Collapsed in the Mates' room and had the rest of the day off. Ginger and I finished off the boat except for "touching up" the paint.

Friday 24th November 1961.
#3 was finished off and we started #2 the motor lifeboat. By the evening we had it completely stripped and all the bottom boards in the well deck in readiness for painting. Lifeboat and fire drill followed in which I again tried out all the breathing apparatus.

Saturday 25th November 1961.
I turned to at 0530 (just about anyway!) and after cleaning the room up I painted the bottom boards and tank cleaning. After lunch I sunbathed, swam and had my haircut by Chang the "Lecky's Mate".

Sunday 26th November 1961.
Today I mostly wrote letters. During the afternoon the sea became rough. We slowed down to tighten the lashings on the mobile workshop that we are carrying for the deck cargo we then

picked up to full ahead.

Monday 27th November 1961.

We continued with the lifeboat today and. Ginge and I painted all of the boat out by about 3 o'clock in the afternoon. We then began to bring all of the buoyancy tanks and bottom boards back up to the boat deck ready to restow to tomorrow.

Tuesday 28th November 1961.

Before breakfast Ginge and I restowed the buoyancy tanks and began on the cleaning. After breakfast, the bosun wanted to "Holy stone" the deck, so all our neatly placed gear was dumped in the lifeboat, and we had to try and put everything back with everything in the boat. We finished off by lunchtime and the Mate gave us the afternoon off.

Wednesday 29th November 1961.

This morning we touched up all the paint in the lifeboat. In the afternoon we checked all of the fire extinguishers with the 4th Mate.

Thursday 30th November 1961.

We arrived in Penang at 0800 and went alongside the wharf. All ships were dressed overall because the King of Malaya or some equally esteemed personage was visiting Penang. I was on day work and watched mail. At 1600 when I knocked off, Tony and I went ashore. That evening, I went ashore with John and Ginge, but we didn't get any further than the seaman's club because the rickshaw men wouldn't take three people, even so we had a nice evening.

Friday 1st December 1961.

At 0700 I went on poop stand-by for leaving the wharf and going to a buoy. The *"Stratheden*[1]*"* was behind us, and I was not at all impressed with her. I was still on day work and my main job was checking Brandy.

Saturday 2nd of December 1961.

Stand-by was at about 07:30 and I was on the pilot ladder. After stand-by the Mate gave us some very welcome time off in which I wrote letters and did office work.

Sunday 3rd of December 1961.
I was woken up by three blasts on the whistle this morning and I went out on deck. Singapore was looking very smart. Just ahead of us in the anchorage was the "*Glenfinlas*[2]". We went on to watches and I was on the 8-12 watch when I had to watch Brandy being unloaded.

Monday 4th December 1961.
I was on day work again and at 0820 I gave Ginge his chow relief from bridge stand-by. By 0830 we were alongside. The watches were split into 7-11, 1-5, 7-11. I was on until 11 and did not have to go on until 1900. Gary Poynter from the "*Menelaus*[3]" phoned up and John, Gray and I all went ashore until about 1700.

Tuesday 5th December 1961.
I worked from 0700 to 1830 and we went on stand-by at 2100 I was on the Poop with the Third Mate.

Wednesday 6th December 1961.
At 0830 I relieved Tony on the bridge and we anchored off the entrance to the river, which leads to Port Swettenham [Renamed Port Klang in July 1972]. We lowered lifeboats #2 and #4. I was in #2 with the Second Mate. We returned at about 11:30. At 1430 we weighed anchor and entered Swettenham. We anchored in the river and began discharging.

Thursday 7th December 1961.
At about 1100 hours we started to go alongside. I was on bridge stand-by. When we were alongside, I was off until 2000. I was then on the 8-12.

Friday 8th December 1961.
I was on daywork and had to do cargo watch #6 as there was some Brandy to be unloaded. That night, Tony and I went ashore

for a swim at the Mariners club with four junior engineers.

Saturday 9th December 1961.

Today we moved to buoy #1 and change places with the "*Orestes*[4]". The captain said, "But for the grace of God is the ship you would have been on". Anyway, we are still on the "*Glenroy*[5]", without, I should think any prospects of our own mail reaching us from now on.

Sunday 10th December 1961.

I was on bridge stand-by from 0545 until 08:30 as we left Swettenham, there was a thick fog. We arrived at Port Dickson at about 1100. We started working cargo at about 1200. Unfortunately, two Middys have to be on, so we're working 6 on, 6 off, and I am on the 6-12 with John.

Monday 11th December 1961.

I turned to at 0600 and did deck watch for one hour when the hatches began working again. Work was finished at 2100 hours, and we sailed immediately. For stand-by I was on the gangway.

Tuesday 12th December 1961.

We were called at 0730 and. After cleaning the room out, we were given the day off. The weather was cold and wet.

Wednesday 13th December 1961.

After being called at 0630, we cleaned the halfdeck out. After breakfast we soogied the bulkheads of the hospital in preparation for painting them. We then painted the deckheads flat white.

Thursday 14th December 1961.

We were called at 0630 and cleared the halfdeck out. We were then given the day off because it was far too rough to paint.

Friday 15th December 1961.

We were called at 0630 and cleared the room out during the morning and part of the afternoon we continued painting the hospital. We were given the rest of the day off. Stand by for Hong

Kong was at 2230 and I was on the gangway.

Saturday 16th December 1961.

At 0830 we weighed anchor and went alongside Holts' Wharf [Sold in 1971, it is now known as Victoria Dockside]. We were secured by 0900. All hatches were working. I was on daywork.

Sunday 17th December 1961.

I was on daywork and turned to at 0630 and cleaned the halfdeck out. During the day I was on deck and did some cargo watching in #2 and #6 where there are some Spirits. Directly after dinner, Tony and I went to the mission for a Carol service. I met a friend off the "*Soudan*[6]" who was at Eskdale with me. After the service there was a buffet supper which satisfied even our voluminous appetites. This was followed by a film called The Lady Killers with Peter Sellers and Alec Guinness. We returned to the ship at about 2300.

Monday 18th December 1961.

I was woken at about 0410 by the 4th Mate to do some cargo watching while Ginge watched mail. At about 0445 the mail was finished so I was able to go back to bed. I was woken again at 0745 and after breakfast started cargo watch. We sailed at 1230 and I was on poop stand-by. We then finished putting brine in the fridge scuppers. We had the rest of the day off.

Tuesday 19th December 1961.

Ginge was on the 8-12, so Tony and I turned to at 0630 on our own and cleaned the room out. Afterwards Tony and I went down #3 and prepared the fridge lockers for freezing. We then redistributed some dunnage. We were given the afternoon off.

Wednesday 20th December 1961.

Tony and I started the hospital again until lunchtime when we heard that the 2nd Mate had been taken ill and a Middy was required on all watches. Tony is now on the 8-12. Watch John the 4-8 and Ginge on the 12-4. I continue with hospital alone.

Thursday 21st December 1961.

Since we left Hong Kong, the weather has been getting worse and now it is cold, and the sea is 'strong breeze'. I turned to 0630, cleaned the room out. I then tested the watertight doors. When this was finished, I continued with the hospital. It is larger than it appears. At 1610 we had a boat drill and fire drill. The 3rd Mate and I changed the compressed air bottle on the breathing apparatus.

Friday 22nd December 1961.

I turned to at 0630 and cleaned the halfdeck out. After breakfast I continued with the hospital, but I was unable to finish it because I had to go on gangway stand-by for Yokohama. We anchored off for about an hour and then went alongside. For going alongside, I was on poop stand by. The weather is sunny and dry but noticeably colder.

Saturday 23rd December 1961.

Ginge, Tony and I were on 6 on 12 off and John was on day work. The first morning we unloaded the Malayan Tin and sheet metal. In the afternoon I went ashore and went up to the Marine tower.

Sunday 24th December 1961.
Christmas Eve.

We sailed at 0930 for Shimizu and apart from stand-bys we had the day off. We reached Shimizu about 1700 and I was on cargo until we sailed at 2330 and I was on poop stand-by.

Monday 25th December 1961,
Christmas Day.

We arrived in Kobe at about 1600 and anchored off to await the Pilot. At about 1800 we went for chow, and we found a jolly good feed awaiting us. Afterwards we had stand-by for going alongside and I was on the gangway. We did not start cargo that night, so we all went ashore.

Tuesday 26th December 1961.
Boxing Day.
We are still working on six on 12 off and I was on the 6-12. Sheet metal was being unloaded painfully slowly. During the morning I helped the 4th Mate with the scuppers. During the afternoon I went ashore and did some shopping.

Wednesday 27th December 1961.
I worked the 12-6 in the morning and we began loading crab and general cargo. This has to be carefully supervised to make sure all of the faces are straight. At 1800 I was on again.

Thursday 28th December 1961.
I was on the 6-12 noon, and we tested wells. After that we filled the deep tanks ready for pressure testing. I had the afternoon off until stand-by at 1730 when I was on the gangway. When we had it hoisted, three more Japanese appeared and naturally wanted to go ashore. We had to hurriedly lower it so they could ashore before our stern drifted out too far. I was then on the 8-12 and stood by the engine room telegraph as we had a Pilot on board going through the Inland Sea.

Friday 29th December 1961.
When I went on watch it to 0830, we were anchored because we were in a snowstorm. By 1900 this had cleared, so we change Pilots and entered the straits of Shimonoseki. I was on engine room telegraph again and by 1230 we were almost clear of the straits. At 2000 I went on watch and my main task was lookout. By 2300 we had just sighted the first light of Quelpart island [Jeju Island] and at 0030, when the 12-4 began because of an hour's clock flog, the second light Mara Tu had just become visible.

Saturday 30th December 1961.
Nothing too much happened on the 8-12 in the morning, but at 2100 we sighted Tsingtao on the port bow, and by 2230 we were anchored, waiting for the quarantine boat and Pilot. At 2300 after a medical inspection of the whole crew, we weighed

anchor and began going alongside the wharf.

Sunday 31st December 1961.

We were alongside by 0045 and then everyone had to muster again and wait in the saloon whilst the search parties went around the ship looking for stowaways. By 0200 this was completed, and we were allowed to go to bed. At 0830 I turned to and watched loading in the fore cabins and then strongrooms. The "wharfies" are ignorant and stubborn. At 1800, the #3 lower hold had been filled and we singled up after being on stand-by for twelve hours. I went on at 2100 and watched in the bridge lockers. By 2345 this was finished.

January 1st 1962.
New Year's Day.

New Year's Day seemed just another day when we were woken up at 0600 to go on muster whilst the ship was searched prior to sailing. Stand-by was at 0720 and I was on the poop. The weather was the same as it has been for the previous three days, high winds, snow showers and temperatures around the lower 20s. At 0810 I was finished on the poop, and I was frozen to the core. At 0835 I went on the bridge to relieve Ginge. At 0910 we dropped the Pilot and at 1150 full speed away was rung down. We are now rolling heavily. The evening watch passed uneventfully.

Tuesday 2nd January 1962.

The 8-12 was mainly uneventful. At 1134 we altered course from 180 degrees to 208 degrees, but the rolling was so bad that we altered again to 190 degrees. We heard this morning that the "*Perseus*[7]" has Hove to.

Wednesday 3rd January 1962.

Nothing eventful happened on the 8-12 and when I went on watch we were in the quarantine anchorage in Hong Kong. we went to buoy A9 at approximately 0900 and by 0915 work had started and I was on deck with the 3rd Mate. At 1400 Ginge and

I went up the Peak and we were back for chow. During the 8-12 I had to do gangway watch as all the Chinese quartermasters had gone ashore.

Thursday 4th January 1962.
Watching the gangway between 8-12 again, nothing eventful happened. I went ashore during the afternoon and did shopping.

Friday 5th January 1962.
Still watching the gangway! No one knows yet what is happening to us. We may leave in Singapore; we may relieve the "*Ascanius*[8]"; we may go home on the "*Glenroy*", Oh to know for sure!

Saturday 6th January 1962.
While I was on the gangway this morning the Padre came aboard and told us B&S had booked rooms at the mission, he was expecting us to go ashore then but still the Mate hasn't heard any definite news, even so he told us to start packing on Sunday.

Sunday 7th January 1962.
Gangway 8-12 and packing 12-8! It doesn't make the job any easier when you think that you will have to unpack everything again in about 24 hours, which will happen if the Captain doesn't hear any definite news.

Monday 8th January 1962.
At 1000, John went to see the captain and came back and told us to be ready to go ashore in ten minutes to sign off. We were ready in five minutes! When we had signed off we learned that we were leaving the "*Glenroy*" at 1600 and we were going to the mission where we would wait an indefinite period for the "*Ulysses*[9]". By 1800 we were installed in the mission for a stay, which turned out to be three weeks.

What We Learnt...

A life on the ocean waves sounds romantic, adventures full of daring do and seeing the wonders of the world as you travel from port to port. You would also think that spending your 17th birthday in the Mediterranean sounds quite good until you realise that you are spending it cleaning and painting. From this voyage you can easily discern that a life at sea, for a midshipman at least, consisted of cleaning, scraping, prepping and then painting various parts of the ship. Interspersed with watching the loading and unloading of cargo.

Something that is brought into sharp relief and not something that we would really consider in this age of instant communication is the disappointment articulated so well within two sentences; is the lack of letters or easy communication from home. For a young lad who had just put to sea and only three days after his seventeenth birthday to put that down in writing in what is ultimately a professional record is a surprisingly hard read.

All that being said, thirteen ports were visited, the first of many Suez Canal transits, and Christmas in Kobe – which sounds like it should be an old Bing Crosby and Bob Hope movie.

S.S. ULYSSES

Masters: R.G. Boyd
                  J. C. Knox
Mates: B. Hill
                  J. K. Marshall
2nd Mates: J. C. Creer
                  J. B. Hodgson
3rd Mate: J. W. Cairns
4th Mates: E. P. Genochio
                  G. Summerfield

<u>Midshipmen</u>
- J. Cummings
- P.J. Delaney
- T. Williamson
- P.J. Wood

"An officer in the Merchant Navy must be able to lead his men by his own practical example and should always be able to show the man how the work should be done. Keep an enquiring mind, therefore, so that you may learn not only how to do a job but also appreciate its significance"

      - *Midshipman Appointment Letter from Alfred Holt & Co. circa 1960*

Voyage of S.S. Ulysses - Map

Voyage Statistics

Monday 29th January 1962 - Hong Kong

Saturday 11th February 1962 - Iloilo (Sugar Wharf)

Monday 13th February 1962 - Cebu

Friday 16th February 1962 - Manila

Sunday 18th February 1962- Hong Kong

Sunday 25th February 1962 - Kobe

Saturday 3rd March 1962 - Nagoya

Thursday 15th March 1962 - San Pedro

Saturday 24th March 1962- Balboa Bay

Panama Canal Transit

Saturday 24th March 1962 - Cristóbal

27th March 1962 – Kingston, Jamaica

31st March 1962 - New York (Bush Terminal)

4th April 1962 - Boston

Wednesday 11th April 1962 - Philadelphia

Thursday 12th April 1962 - Baltimore

Wednesday 18th April 1962 - Beaumont (End of Voyage 31)

Thursday 19th April 1962 - Houston

Sunday 22nd April 1962 - Lake Charles

Tuesday 24th April 1962 - New Orleans

Saturday 28th April 1962 - Newport News

Sunday 29th April 1962 - Philadelphia

Monday 20th April 1962 - New York

Wednesday 16th May 1962 - Alexandria

17th May 1962 - Port Said

Suez Canal Transit

21st May 1962 - Djibouti

31st May 1962 - Penang

1st June 1962 - Port Swettenham (Port Klang)

5th June 1962 - Singapore

10th June 1962 - Bangkok

16th June 1962 - Djakarta (Jakarta - Tanjung Priok)

20th June 1962 - Surabaya

27th June 1962 - Sungai Gerong

30th June 1962 - Pladju

6th July 1962 - Hong Kong (Taikoo Dockyard)

Total number of Ports visited: 34
Total Voyage time: 158 days
Total Voyage Distance*: 36,898 Nautical miles

* All distances are estimated using Reed's New Maritime Distance Tables (1965) [Acquired from Fenton Steamship Co. Chartering and S&P department] and by going "old school" with Lloyds Atlas of World Shipping Ports (30th Edition). Ports, wharfs, jetties and buoys have all changed dramatically over the last 62 years so that calculating accurate distances is nearly impossible to determine, so we used our best judgement.

Monday 29th January 1962.
Hong Kong

We were woken up at 0730 so that we could be at Taikoo dockyard by 0930. After breakfast we did our own last-minute packing and by 0855 all our own gear was aboard the lorry. We were met in a taxi, and we left the mission with faces as long as the day is long.

We arrived at Taikoo at approx. 0915 and we could see a bluey anchored off. We waited and waited and finally at 1300 she began to come to the dry dock. It was very interesting watching her drydock and by 1445 we were aboard – Phew! By 1700 we had unpacked and now we had to scrub out. After chow we reviewed our position and considered it favourable - the Mates and the others all seem nice chaps. At 2000 John, Ginge and I went ashore.

Tuesday 30th January 1962.

We were woken by the doctor at 0720 this morning. After chow, John, Ginge and I looked around the ship to find our own way about. Tony was cleaning up the halfdeck and was there if any of the Mates wanted him. During the afternoon I had to make sure dunnage was stowed correctly in #2 and #4. The noise and bustle of board is terrific, and the ship looks in a sorry state. It will be a wonder if she is finished within a month, let alone six days.

Wednesday 31st January 1962 - Saturday 3rd February.

Work is now going at alarming rate. We have nothing in particular to do, but we look around at all the jobs that are being done and, in this way, I for one, am finding a lot out about the ship. Among the things. We have looked at are the inside of the boilers, inside the steam tail, the top of the funnel, inside the double bottom, in the cable lockers and a small generator turbine. On Saturday we shifted from the dry dock to the wharf. Stand-by was at 1115 and we were secure by 1200. I was on bridge stand-by.

Sunday 4th February 1962 - Wednesday 7th February '62.

We moved to a buoy #134 and stand-by was at 0900 hours and we were secure by 11:15. I was again on the bridge. No major repairs are taking place, just painting and chipping. We are on daywork and have painted the dodgers, and we are now sooging the boat deck. Stand-by for leaving Hong Kong was at 0100 hours. I was on daywork.

Thursday 8th February - Saturday 11th February.

I have now started sooging the rails on the ladders to paint later. We sighted the Philippines at about 2000 Thursday. On Saturday we arrived in Iloilo. We had stand-by at 0630 and I was on gangway. We anchored off the Sugar wharf at 0730. After chow at 0900 we had the stand-by for going alongside and once more I was on the gangway. We are all fast by 1036. During the afternoon we swept out #2 and #4 in preparation for the sugar. We then had to paste up down #2. At 1930 we had to shift ship so the sugar could be loaded into #2. Stand-by was finished by 2130 and again we went down #2 to finish pasting up. We knocked off about 2230 and I had done 18 hours work that day. Lower hold #2 was filled during Sunday night, so we shifted back to #4. Stand-by was over by 1009.

Sunday 12th February - Saturday 17th February.

The sugar was loaded by 1600 and stand-by was at 1630. I was on the gangway. The Pilot left about 1740. We arrived in Cebu about 0800 and the wharf was right next to the road. We loaded oil and some general cargo. During the morning we carried on with soogieing and after lunch we all went out in the motor lifeboat under the 3rd Mate. The weather was very hot. On Wednesday we were called at 0600 and I cleaned out the room. After breakfast we began painting the fiddley awning spas. The other three had the afternoon off whilst I carried on painting. Stand-by was at 1915 for leaving and I was on the gangway. On Thursday I carried on painting.

On Friday morning we arrived in Manila at 0640 and we

anchored in the harbour, we carried on painting the fiddley we had the afternoon and the evening off. During the evening John injured his foot and is now laid up.

Saturday we were called at 0600 hrs whilst I cleaned the room out the other two painted on the fiddley and boat deck. Again, we had the afternoon off. Stand-by for leaving was at 1930 and I was on the bridge. F.S.A. was at 2100.

Sunday 18th February - Saturday 24th February.
Hong Kong - Kobe.
I was on daywork, and we were painting the fiddely after smoko I went onto the bridge in readiness for entering Hong Kong. We were on full speed right until 5 minutes before the Pilot so we would not be late. We picked up the Pilot at 1130, and at 11:45 we anchored for quarantine. After half an hour we weighed anchor and headed for our buoy, we were fast at 1312. We had the rest of the day off and Ginge and I went ashore. The following day we were called for breakfast. Afterwards we spent the day Soogieing the foc'sle head. We had Wednesday off but we crashed in the afternoon as we would notably be required for night watches. I did the 12-4 and did mostly measuring up.

We left Hong Kong at 0715 Thursday and I was on the gangway. When we had left we finished soogieing and began painting the foc'sle head. When we were nearing Kobe, we were put on watches, I was on the 4-8. It is getting much cooler now; the temperature is 40 degrees Fahrenheit.

Sunday 25th February - Saturday 3rd March.
Kobe - Nagoya.
On Sunday evening we were approaching Kobe, it was quite foggy and a good look out was kept for small fishing vessels, which don't seem to be able to afford lights. Stand-by was at 1736. We anchored at 1933 we were not going in until the morning because the customs had finished for the day. We went alongside at 0750 and by 0902 we were fast at pier 5. We then carried on with the foc'sle head. I went ashore that night.

Tuesday morning we were called at 0730 and we continued with the foc'sle head. Stand-by for leaving was at 2300 and I was on the gang way.

On Wednesday afternoon at 1451 we arrived in Nagoya and at 1615 we were all fast, for a change I was on the gangway. They finished cargo for the night at 8 O'clock and would not be starting again until the next day. I went to bed early. The next day it was drizzling but they worked cargo. During the evening there was to be a shippers party so we hung flags up and generally prepared the area on the boat deck and smoke room. We went ashore that evening with the 2nd Spark. On Saturday we sailed at 0136 and I was on the gangway. Then started our trip across the Pacific. We had most of the weekend off.

Sunday 4th March - Thursday 15th March.
Nagoya - San Pedro.

I started my office work in earnest today so that it would be ready for marking at San Pedro. On Monday Ginge, Tony and I were on day work whilst John was on the 12-4, we will now be doing the 12-4 in weekly rota basis. Ginge will be on next week, I will do the week after and Tony the last week of the month. Every morning now we climb the foremast at nine o'clock then we have a signals exercise sending morse from the after end of the fiddly to the poop. We have now started chipping the poop in readiness for painting. There is a very heavy swell running, but we have not encountered any really bad weather yet.

On Tuesday we put red lead on all masts that had been chipped and two of us were put on the captain's bedroom which we had to paint with "Leatherette" paint. This is extremely difficult to put on because it is very thick and does not appear to cover the surface until it is dry. The room when we had finished was in three tones of blue and it looked quite good.

Thursday the eighth was the day that we crossed the International Dateline. This meant we had two Thursdays the eighths. On the second Thursday, I received telegram from my brother telling me that my father had died the day before. This shook me rigid, but I find working hard helps to take my mind off it. All my spare time is taken up with office work now and I am certainly "knocking a hole" in it. There is still some swell, but we have not had any really bad weather yet. Ginge went onto the 12-4 on Sunday and he had to do the daylight watch. During the next week, we continued with our office work, mast climbing and signals.

Our job was now to finish cutting in on the poop and paint all the bollards black. We also cut in on the fiddly. This was finished and then we started to paint all of the lifebuoys and lifebuoy lights, for this we rigged up on a heaving line between the two derricks on #4 and then hung the lifebuoys on that. As we were doing this the first land since Japan came into view and it was very reassuring to see "Terra Nova". The temperature now became pleasantly warm. I was put on the 4-8 and it was a very nice feeling to see the hills of California instead of the Blue Pacific. We picked up the Pilot at about 1900 and by 0830 we were alongside the wharf. The first job was to go through "immigration" who was in fact a very pleasant chap, who called us by our own Christian names, and by 2200 we all had our passes and after reading our mail we crashed.

Friday 16th March.
San Pedro.
We had the morning off and John, Tony and I went to shore. Tony went into Los Angeles while John and I stayed in Wilmington. We managed to change some Japanese yen and Hong Kong dollars and we had a good look around. We returned to the ship for lunch and afterwards I had the afternoon off until stand-by at 1700 hours. I was on gangway and we dropped the Pilot about 1800 hours.

Saturday 17th March - Saturday 24th March.
San Pedro - Balboa.
On Saturday morning we just did a few odd jobs around the ship and had the afternoon off. Now that the office work has

been sent in there seems to be a lot of time on our hands, but I have started a book called Hawaii which will keep me quiet for a while. On Sunday I started on the 12-4 at nighttime and daywork during the afternoon. On Monday afternoon the 3rd Mate came down and checked all the lifeboat stores. It took the rest of the afternoon to repack the stores.

On Tuesday morning we were out of bearings, so I took a sight and in the afternoon I helped Tony grease some lifeboat tanks in #1 boat. The difficult part is replacing the tanks after they have been greased, they seemed to be the wrong shape. The weather is much hotter now and working in the boats is hot work. The tanks took two hard days to do, and when they were finished we began to overhaul all the gear in the boat. We changed the batteries in the torches, greased all the shackles and blocks, overhauled the pumps, refilled the petrol tanks, greased the davit head spans, greased the stays.

When this was completed, we had to replace all the lifeboat grab lines and lifelines. When we had only done half the job we ran out of rope and had to use any other suitable rope we could find. Then we had to make sure all the boats had at least one heel grab line and all the lifelines. This meant that we had to work overtime in a semi-tropical rainstorm, a disaster.

The next day we arrived in Balboa Bay and we anchored to await to the Pilot.

Saturday 24th March.
Panama Canal transit.
0915 we weighed anchor and went into the canal through the port of Balboa. I was on the poop for stand-by. At 1015 we were approaching the 'Miraflores' locks. At 1030 the "mules" were fast aft and we were towed into the first lock.

Panama Canal

We were raised about 20 to 30 feet in about 5 minutes and then we were towed into the second lock where we were again raised very quickly. We had risen about 60 feet in the space of 20 minutes. The next locks were about half an hour steaming time away and here we had to wait for our turn. At 1230 when I relieved John on the bridge we were already in the first of the two locks.

When we left the 'Pedro Miguel' Locks we entered a cut in the hill, which could have only been about 500 foot wide. At 1357 we were able to work up to full sea revs to go through the lakes. At 1545 we slowed down to anchor in Gatún Lake, where we would have to wait for a new Pilot. I was crashed when we went through the Gatun Locks, but by 2300 we were all fast in Cristóbal.

25th of March to the 27th of March.
Cristóbal to Kingston.
On Sunday we sailed from Cristóbal at 1030 and I was on the gangway. At about 1200 we dropped the Pilot and we had the rest of the day off. On Monday we were all on day work, in which time we completed painting the lifeboat oilcans, finishing the

grab lines and generally tidying up the boat. For stand-by on Tuesday morning, for entering Kingston, I was on the poop. By 0745 we were all fast on Pier 7.

27th March 1962.
Kingston

I was on deck during the morning and we were discharging in #1, #2, #3 and #4. By 1730 cargo had finished and so at 1830, I went on the bridge. Then started to search for stowaways. This took about an hour and at about 1930 I was relieved on the bridge by Ginge.

Kingston – New York.
27th March to 31st March.

I went on the 8-12 but on Wednesday morning we could not have signals because the bottom of the battery box fell out, what a pity! We then replaced the first aid kits in the lifeboats and covered the lifeboats. Our job from now on was to Soogi all the white paint except on the forward side of the bridge and after end of the accommodation.

I remained on 8-12 during the nighttime. As we entered New York, after picking up the Pilot about 1330, we had to wash down the focs'le head to get rid of the soogi stains. We were anchored at quarantine from about 1545 until 1745 and then we headed for Bush Terminal Pier 2. We were alongside by 1830. I was on the gangway and to my surprise an uncle, whom I had never seen, was one of the first people aboard. As it was the weekend and no cargo was to be worked the Mate gave me until Monday morning off, something which I shall always appreciate.

New York.
31st March - 3rd April.

On Saturday night I went ashore with my uncle [Uncle Bert] about 1900 and by eight o'clock we were at his house in Staten Island. We went out for chow that night and I had a terrific steak. Next day he took me to his shop where he insisted on loading me up with books and writing paper. In the afternoon we went for a tour of New York. We ended up at the U.N. where we went on a guided tour. This took about an hour and was exceedingly interesting. After we had finished there we drove around some more and then went back home. The next morning, April 2nd, I left my uncle's house at 0730 and was back aboard by 0845. I was not on until 12. When I went on #1, #2, #3, #4 and #5 were being unloaded. At 1700 #5 was finished. The shore gangs then knocked off until the next day. That night I again went ashore to my uncles returning to the ship about 2200.

1830 Tuesday we sailed for Boston and for stand-by I was on poop.

New York - Boston.
4th April 1962.

At 2000, on the 3rd I went on the bridge, we had just dropped the Pilot when I went on the bridge. At about 0400 on the 4th we entered the Cape Cod Canal and we left there about 0700. We picked up a Boston Pilot at 1030 from a sailing pilot vessel, at 1200 we were alongside. John and I had some time off so we went ashore. We thought Boston was very good and at 2000 we were back aboard and I went on watch. By 2315 Cargo was finished. At 2345 we tested the gear. Stand-by was at 0015. I was on the poop.

Thursday 5th April - Wednesday 11th April.
Boston - Philadelphia.

I remained on the 8-12 and at 2345 Thursday we picked up the Pilot for the Delaware River. By the time I was called the next day we had nearly reached the wharf. For stand-by I was on the gangway. As soon as we were alongside cargo was started and very soon it was finished. We then shifted ship to the sugar wharf, where we stayed until Monday without starting the sugar. At 0800 Monday the sugar started but we were on daywork.

I had done the night, so I had the morning off. Monday afternoon saw us scraping #2 and #4 tween decks to remove all the excess sugar. Tuesday morning we sugied the half rounds. Stand-by for leaving Philadelphia was at 1030 Wednesday.

Philadelphia – Baltimore.
I was in daywork and had to shift cargo mats. We went through the Chesapeake and Delaware Canal. We left the canal at 1720 and by 2030 we were alongside. I was on the gangway. We immediately started discharging oil and by 2200 I crashed.

Baltimore - Beaumont.
Friday 13th April – Noon Wednesday 18th April.
I was on daywork for the first part of this trip and I cleaned out the hatches and laid dunnage. We passed extremely close to Miami and shortly after rounding the tip of Florida, we changed into whites. We picked up the Pilot at 0700 on Wednesday morning and the stand-by up the river was about 5 hours. In the river there were several blocks of laid up ships. There were about 200 ships in all. The Americans claimed to be able to get all of them to sea in two months. I wouldn't like to sail in them. For going alongside the Sulphur wharf I went on the poop. We were alongside by 1200. Here Voyage 31 ended.

Noon 18th April – Thursday 19th April.
Beaumont – Houston.
600 tons of bulk sulphur was loaded in the "phenomenal" time 35 minutes and at 1500 we shifted ship to the oil wharf where we were to load lubricating oil for Java. I was on the bridge for stand-by and then at 1600 I went on the gangway. During the night 12-4 we pressure tested the double bottom and commenced loading the oil. At 0800 the next morning that was finished and at 1050 we sailed for Houston. At 1545 we dropped the Pilot and we headed for Houston. By midnight we were alongside. I was on poop stand-by and the river stank.

Houston – Lake Charles.
Friday 20th April – Sunday 22nd April.
In Houston, we loaded mainly rice into #1, #2 and #5. Some

machinery was put in #2. During the morning John and I went ashore and had a look at the shops. During the afternoon 12-4 we loaded two heavy lifts into #2 tween deck. Mainly we were testing scuppers. When I went to ask the Mate if I could go ashore I landed myself with the job of sweeping the mud into the hat boxes of the deep tanks. This took until 1815. I missed chow and did not go ashore. I was not required for morning 12-4 and we sailed at 1500.

I put down on the chart as usual and at 1600 when John relieved me, we were about 7 miles from the wharf. At about 1730 we passed the "Lone Star Monument" and the *"Battleship Texas*[10]*"*. By 2024 we had left the river. We picked up the Pilot for Lake Charles about 0045 and we entered the river about 0100. I was on the 12-4 and again I kept her going on the chart. About 0600 we were alongside. John and I went ashore during the morning and despite the fact that it was Easter Sunday, we were still able to find some shops open. We returned to the ship for lunch. We sailed at 2130 and for stand-by I was on the poop.

Battleship Texas

Monday 23rd April – Tuesday 24th April.
Lake Charles – New Orleans.

At 1630 we went on stand-by for going up the Mississippi. I was on daywork and had been packing some of the Mates boxes for him. At about 0130 Tuesday I was called to go on gangway stand-by. We were alongside and clewed up by 0206. I was in bed by 0216. I was given the day off until we sailed, John and I went ashore in the morning and we were very favourably impressed by the town. We went up Canal Street and we were able to see down the famous Bourbon Street. We returned to the ship for lunch and we sailed at 1630, by 2230 we had left the great Mississippi behind.

Wednesday 25th April – Saturday 28th April.
New Orleans – Newport News.

I was on a daywork packed some more of the Mates gear. We then started cleaning the tween decks of #2 and #5 in readiness for a rat inspection in Newport News. We were able to put the swimming pool up and one morning the Mate told us to go for a swim at 7 o'clock. At 0624 on Saturday we picked up the Pilot and by 0915 we were alongside. During our short stay we loaded tobacco in #1 and #5. We sailed at 1400 and I was on the poop. I was on the 8-12 and at 0100 we picked up the Delaware river Pilot. At 0745 we were alongside.

Sunday 29th April – Monday 30th April.
Philadelphia – New York.

We loaded general in #2, #4 and #5 and at 1600 we sailed from Philadelphia and at 2100 we left the river and almost immediately we ran into fog. I was then given the job of blowing the whistle at intervals not exceeding two minutes for an interval of from 4 to 6 seconds. At 0730 I was called to go on the poop for entering New York and at 0255 we were all fast.

Monday 30th April – Wednesday 2nd May.
New York.

As one was required on deck at 1300, I went ashore to see my uncle, returning the following morning at 0730. I again went on deck and at 1230 I wanted to go ashore; I was unable to because the passes hadn't arrived. At 1630 when the passes did arrive I went ashore with the 2nd Carpenter and we ended up at the pictures. We returned to the ship about 0130. The new Mate is on board now and so is the Chief Engineer. We sailed at 2130 on Wednesday when I did the 8-12. We discharged the Pilot at 2400.

Thursday 3rd May – Wednesday 16th May.
New York – Alexandria.

I am still on the 8-12 and now take a morning and a noon sight. The dayworker, or one of them has to take stars. Whilst working during the mornings we had to work out stability tables. The new system has crystallised now, whereby the 8-12 and the 12-4 Middy's each take a morning and a noon sight, all Middies go on to the bridge at 1 o'clock for half hour quiz and then in the evening one of the dayworkers take stars. At weekend the daylight 12-4's are worked by the 12-4 Middy. We should soon be proficient at sights and principles.

On Sunday we were not called and we missed breakfast. On Monday John and I finished off the stability tables and gave them to the Mate. I took stars Monday night and managed to get a reasonable answer. Tuesday saw us checking paint and stores on the ship which took quite a while. Wednesday was also checking stores. On Thursday we cleaned out the boat deck lockers and the Quartermaster's locker. During Friday we passed Gibraltar at 1730, which means that we have been round the world once.

The weather was getting a bit rough as we left the Atlantic, but now in the Mediterranean seems okay! On Saturday we overhauled the shackles on the davit spans and Stockholm tarred the davit spans. We had the afternoon off. On Sunday we were not called again, but this time made breakfast. I did the 12-4 in the afternoon when we passed the "*Agapenor*[11]" who was taking D.F. bearings on us. We passed a lot of other ships as well, mainly during the night 12-4 and I was able to do some morse practice in signalling to these ships. The weather is extremely pleasant and at night the sea is flat calm, with a bright moon and a slight haze. Stand-by for Alexandria was at 1200 and at 1230 I went on the bridge and relieved John. We went in almost straight away and were anchored in the harbour by 1327.

Alexandria.
16th May.
Cargo started immediately and we had two heavy lifts as well as a lot of general. Ginge and I had to measure the freeboard.

Alexandria – Port Said.
16th – 17th May.
We left Alexandria at 2100 and I was in my bunk for stand-by. When I went on the 12-4 we were at Nelson Island, where the famous Battle of the Nile was fought by Nelson. The night was very clear and there were a lot of ships. The 2nd Mate showed me how to turn on the radar and use same. The watch past extremely quickly and the radar is still in working order.

Port Said and Canal transit.
17th May – 18th May.
I was called at 0730 to go on noon stand-by. We eventually went in about 0840 and we were moored in the anchorage by 1000. Cargo started at about 12:30 and I had to tally specials out of #2 strongroom. We also loaded oranges in #3 D.T. and potatoes in #5 D.T. I was called at 1115 to go on bridge stand-by. We were the fourth ship into the canal and we went in at about 0006. All I had to do the whole watch was keep a lookout. The 2nd Mate kept us going on the chart. We entered the cut at about 3 o'clock. At 0400 we had nearly reached the lakes. We were anchored in the lakes to let the northbound convoy pass until 1100. When I went on the bridge at 1230, we weren't very far from the exit of the canal. We thought that we were going to have to anchor to unload one case, a large refrigerator, but the Pilot said that we could unload whilst underway onto a tug. Full speed away was at 1500. By 1600 it seemed that only one ship, a

tanker, was overtaking us. We had boat drill.

Suez – Djibouti.
18th May – 21st May.

On the 12-4 that night one other ship appeared to be catching up with us. We found that it was the "*Oranje*[12]". and with only one alter course during the watch not much happened. At the weekend I went on daywork with John and we had to overhaul the lifeboat lead blocks. Quite an easy but messy job. We also checked all the fall blocks to make sure they swivelled. On Monday we arrived in Djibouti about midnight. I was on the gangway. At 0540 stand-by went for going alongside I was on the gangway. We were alongside by 0610.

Djibouti.
22nd May.

Cargo started immediately and we unloaded drums from #3, a heavy lift from #4 and some general from #5. I was on accommodation patrol with John. I did Tony and Ginge's smoko reliefs down #3 where they were watching to check that no oranges were pinched. I went on the bridge for stand-by and full speed away was at 1620.

Djibouti – Penang.
22nd May – 31st May.

We worked on #4 boat for the first few days, scraping, cleaning and painting it. Again, we came across the difficulty of the buoyancy tanks, which are not easy to replace. We were interrupted by a great deal of rain squalls and these held up the painting. As we were in the S.W. monsoon we passed to the north of Socotra and we had about a nine-hour break from the bad weather. I have now done nearly ten hours on the wheel for my steering certificate and the bad weather doesn't make the job any easier.

The lifeboats are metal and are far easier to paint than those on the "*Glenroy*". I went on the 8-12 on Sunday night and we passed South of Ceylon [Known as Sri Lanka since 1972]. We dropped

Ceylon during the 8-12 on Monday evening and from then on not much happened. On the 30th we picked up Pulo Weh [Pulau We] and on the 8-12 the following evening. I had to take the wheel for a short while on stand-by because the quartermaster was caught out with diarrhoea or something. We anchored by 2400, cargo started immediately. I was off for the whole time in port.

Penang – Port Swettenham.
1st June.
Stand-by to weigh anchor was at 0900 and I went on the bridge. We went out via the south channel which was interesting because Blue Funnel ships do not often go that way. The stand-by was longer but it cut about an hour and a half off the steaming time. When I went on the 8-12 in the evening we were in the river. At 2040 we anchored off where they are building the new wharves.

Port Swettenham.
1st June – 5th June.
On Saturday June 2nd the Middies were going to start a launch service from the ship to the shore in the motor lifeboat. We took out the mast and sails and one or two oars and then sugied the boat out. We lowered it into the water and went for a short trip around the ship. Alas, the boats water cooling pump was not working so the Mate had to order a shoreside launch service hence we had the weekend off apart from shifting ship. We left the anchorage at 1745 and were secure to buoy #2 at 1840. On Sunday the 2nd Mate had his birthday so a whole lot of us went ashore and had a good time. On Monday morning we moved alongside to discharge the heavy lifts but at 1730 we moved back to the buoys to complete the discharge. On the 5th at 0330 we sailed and I went on the foc'sle head.

Port Swettenham – Singapore.
5th of June.
John and I were on day work for this short journey and we

tidied up the halfdeck and completed some cargo plans which we had started earlier. Early in the morning we put some dangerous cargo on #3 hatch to be unloaded before we reached Singapore. We anchored at 1612 to drop this off onto a Lighter and by 1630 we were away again. I went down to the engine room for stand-by at 1700 and at 1800 we were alongside, ahead of the "*Menelaus*".

Singapore.
5th – 8th June.

I stayed aboard the first night and answered my mail. The greatest shock we had was when John's father wrote and told him that we were being relieved by the "*Ajax*[13]" in Hong Kong. I'm sure they are pleased about this at home, but I personally would rather do one more trip. Cargo started in earnest the next day and at the beginning there were two on deck. On the 7th it was changed to one on deck by the 2nd Mate which we all appreciated. All hatches were working until Thursday when they covered up #4 and #2. From #4 they unloaded tractors which were finished that night. Cargo finished at 1030 the following day. We sailed immediately and had left the wharf at 1112. I was on the poop for stand-by.

Singapore – Bangkok.
8th June – 10th June.

When we were in the Eastern Road we anchored to pick up our dangerous cargo again, full speed away was at 1218. In the afternoon John and I cleaned out the halfdeck and then continued with cargo plans. The next morning John and I put up the swimming pool between us and Tony scraped the lifeboat blocks. We had Saturday afternoon at sea and I did some office work to be sent in in Hong Kong. I was on the 12-4 when we anchored at the Bangkok bar at 1400 to await the tide. We did not move in until 0200 the next morning.

Bangkok.
10th June – 12th June.

I was called at 0130 and we weighed anchor at 0200. At 0230 the steering gear appeared to be going wrong, so I was told to get two red lights up with the quartermaster ready for lighting. I collected the streamers from the chartroom and then I could only find one red bulb. I found the Lecky and we went down to his shop to find a bulb. When we got there it took him quite a while to find a bulb with the right connector. When I returned to the bridge, I expected to find the steamer all ready for hoisting, but no. I could not even find the streamer, the quartermaster had not put it up. Eventually I found it by the binnacle and hurried to hoist it up. Now someone was blowing "D" on the whistle – . . I could hardly think for the noise, I was sweating cobs. The Second Mate was shouting at me to hand him the plug. Eventually after about 30 seconds, which seemed like 30 minutes the lights were up and burning brightly phew!!

I then rushed down to the bridge and saw about half a cable from the starboard bow another smaller vessel bearing down on us. We let go our starboard anchor at 0312 and this just swung us clear off the other vessel, which was now discernible as a dredger. We then hove up the anchor and continued on our way. At 0400 we were just about to anchor to await the right tide. I was called at 0715 to go on stand-by for'ard for mooring off the wharves at Bangkok.

During the afternoon 12-4 I leaded the lifeboat blocks with Tony. At 1700 we went alongside and I was again on the foc'sle for stand-by. They worked #4 strong room during the night 12-4 and I was down there tallying whilst Tony watched the mosphice down there. We missed the tide the next day, so we moved out to the river again and moored. At 2100 we started down the river. On the night 12-4, I was so tired that I did not get on the bridge until 0020 when we had just left the bar.

Bangkok – Djakarta (Tanjung Priok)
12th June – 16th June.

For this trip I remained on the 12-4 and did many things such as taking a sight of the Moon and Venus. On the 15th during the

12-4 we approach the Bangka strait. We passed through between 1700 and 2200 with the engines on stand-by. During the 12-4 that night nothing of any note happened and the next morning at 1100 we anchored off the breakwater to await the Pilot. We were alongside by 1230. I was on the foc'sle head for stand-by.

Djakarta.
16th June – 18th June.
Whilst here we worked 6 on, 12 off with one on daywork. The cargo was mainly bagged rice from #5. The *"Antilochus*[14]*"* was just astern of us and we went ashore a couple of times with the Middies off her. On the 17th we moved to the Coal Wharf to unload the lub oil into road tankers. The *"Tantalus*[15]*"* came in whilst we were here and she went down to Holt's Wharf. We sailed for Surabaya on the 18th at 2140. I was on the foc'sle head for stand-by.

Djakarta – Surabaya.
18th June – 20th June.
John and I oiled mooring wires the following day and after the first one we ran out of oil. The bosun mixed up another mess and we finished off another two with that. We were reduced for the whole trip to have a daylight arrival.

Surabaya.
20th June – 25th June.
We anchored to await the Pilot who was supposed to arrive at 0630 but did not come until 1230. I was down the engine room for stand-by for a short while because of the stand-by itself is a long one. We were eventually moored by 1515 alongside Holt's Wharf. We went on six hours watches, except between 2300 and 0700 when they weren't working cargo, when one of us did the night. The *"Antilochus"* arrived a day later and we were all pleased until we found out three of the Middies were laid up with food poisoning. The cargo to be discharged was nearly all rice in all holds. Some lamp black was unloaded from #6.

On Friday, Tony and I along with the Mate, 2nd Engineer, 6th and 7th Engineers and 2nd Electrician and Chief Sparks all went to the swimming pool at Mount Tretes. Tony and I were the only two to risk a ride on the horses, something which I enjoyed very much indeed.

We sailed eventually on the 25th at 1150.

Surabaya – Sungai Gerong
25th June – 27th June.

The Pilot left at 1400 and I was on the 8-12. The following day during the 12-4 we entered the Bangka Strait for the second time. When I knocked on the 8-12, we had not very far to go to the Musi River. We anchored at 2200 to await the Pilot. Not knowing when the Pilot would come, the 3rd Mate knocked me off. I was nearly crashed when the Pilot came aboard, so I returned to the bridge "Post Haste". The anchor was away by 2248 and we proceeded up the river. How the Pilot knew where he was going is something beyond my comprehension. There are only a few lights every now and again we anchored about 0400.

Sungai Gerong.
27th June – 30th June.

I was called at 0630 to do the foc'sle stand-by. Cargo started immediately and we work 6 on, 12 off. They did not work nights and John and Ginge did them between them. The cargo here was mainly Chevrolet trunk trucks and odds and ends of refinery gear. Sungai Gerong is actually a Stanvac oil refinery [an American joint venture by Standard Oil of New Jersey and Socony-Vacuum Oil (aka Mobil) established in 1931. The company went defunct in 1962].

Sungai Gerong – Pladju.
30th of June.

Stand-by was over chow time and although it is just a shift ship it took from 1745 until 1900. We used our starboard anchor to swing on and it seemed possible to jump from the poop into the Pladju mariners club swimming pool. Tony came up after he had his chow to relieve me, and then I relieved John.

Pladju.

30th June – 2nd July.

We were unloading the sulphur here, which was the first cargo we loaded at the beginning of the voyage and is last out. It took 35 minutes to load but two days, 18 hours to discharge. The discharge was done with an antiquated grab which worked properly for only 50 percent of the time. We had to keep a fire watch down the hatch and for us we were given gas masks of ultra-modern design. With two hoses into the lower hold and every now and again we dump them down.

We eventually sailed at 1700 on the second, sick of the sight and smell of sulphur. We were full away by 2315.

Pladju – Hong Kong.

2nd July – 6th July.

John and I were on daywork and we changed the lifeboat ladder on #2 boat. We sugied the boats and davits and all the white on the fiddely. On Thursday we finished some cargo plans and Friday John and I gave the halfdeck a thorough clean. For arrival in Hong Kong I went on the foc'sle head and we anchored at 2230 for quarantine. It felt like arriving home to see all the lights again and I was doubly made-up because I received plenty of mail. We finally anchored off Taikoo dockyard at 2330.

Hong Kong.

7th July - 12th July.

I was called at 0630 to go on stand-by but when I was up there was no stand-by to do. We waited all morning and eventually moved alongside at 1230. I was on the bridge for stand-by. We did not use the engines and we were taken by two tugs alongside. The Mate wants us on deck all the time and we worked sea watches until midnight. I did the 4-8 after which I went ashore to see the Alamo. On Saturday I did the afternoon watch and merely kept an eye on all that was going on. We had a lunch picnic on Sunday afternoon, followed by chow at the Padres.

Monday I did the morning and we heard from the Mate that we would be changing ship at 1500. I finish packing and was all ready at 1500. The launch arrived at 1600 and we were on board the "*Ajax*" by 1730.

What We Learnt...

And what have we learnt after this second voyage? Well, the transcribing of the voyage turned out to be a lot more difficult than I first expected. The handwriting for one got progressively worse as the tiredness crept in over the 158 days of the voyage. However, during the transcribing of this voyage, I finally realised just how young and how far from home my dad was when he heard about his own father's death, via telegram. On his second Thursday 8th March of 1962, after crossing the international date line. I couldn't imagine being aged seventeen, in the middle of the Pacific Ocean and being told he had died. And in the log the stoic phase "it shook me rigid" and then the rest of the log entry talks about work and watches taken. I am very thankful that I have had 46 years with him.

It was easier to plot the course on the map with this log as rather than individual day entries with ports mentioned in the text, each leg and port were written up separately.

The midshipmen continue to be the general dogs' bodies of the ship, checking stores, painting, office work and testing the lifeboats. We had a bit of drama with the failing steering gear which shows that all the maintenance that they have been doing is required and I worked out where I got my dry sense of humour from on this voyage though.

So, we had the first full circumnavigation of the globe for Midshipman P. J. Wood, Crossing the international date line (cool), transiting not only the Suez Canal but also the Panama Canal – all done before the age of 18 no less! Not sure what I had managed to achieve before the age of 18, but it wasn't half of that – now I come to think of it, I also know where my slight inferiority complex and need to impress my dad also comes from...

M.V. AJAX

July 1962

Master: A.C. Sparks
Mate: J. T. H. Bennion
2nd Mate: T. S. Main
3rd Mate: T. A. Beggs
4th Mate: I. W. Lawrenson

<u>Midshipmen</u>
- J. Cummings
- P.J. Delaney
- T. Williamson
- P.J. Wood
- A. N. Wilson
- D. B. Ridall

"The carriage of goods between different parts of the world is the first and foremost function of the Merchant Navy and the Managers attach the highest importance to the skill and care shown by their officers in the safe and efficient performance of this duty."

- *Midshipman Appointment Letter from Alfred Holt & Co. circa 1960*

Voyage of M.V. Ajax - Map

Voyage Statistics

12th July 1962 - Hong Kong

20th July 1962 - Otaru

Tuesday 24th July 1962 - Hsin Kang (Tianjin Xingang)

31st July 1962 - Kobe

Sunday 12th August 1962 - Manilla

Wednesday 15th August 1962 - Hong Kong

Monday 27th August 1962 - Singapore

Monday 3rd September 1962 - Penang *(Medical Emergency - Crew mate picked up by Pilot boat)*

Friday 14th September 1962 - Aden

Suez Canal Transit

Tuesday 18th September 1962 - Port Said

Friday 26th September 1962 - Liverpool

Total number of Ports visited: 11
Total Voyage time: 76 days
Total Voyage Distance*: 13,819 Nautical miles

* All distances are estimated using Reed's New Maritime Distance Tables (1965) [Acquired from Fenton Steamship Co. Chartering and S&P department] and by going "old school" with Lloyds Atlas of World Shipping Ports (30th Edition). Ports, wharfs, jetties and buoys have all changed dramatically over the last 62 years so that calculating accurate distances is nearly impossible to determine, so we used our best judgement.

Hong Kong.
12th July.

As soon as we were aboard, we began unpacking. After chow I was on with Tony. This was the first actual Blue Funnel ship I've worked on and suddenly different from both the *"Glenroy"* and the *"Ulysses"*. The next day during the evening. Ike, John and I went to a barbeque organised by the mission. We returned about 2330. At 0300 I was called to go on the night whilst Ginge stood by. There was a typhoon warning and two of us had to be ready. During Wednesday I ordered a red brocade waistcoat. I did the night Thursday morning.

We sailed at 1200 and I was on the foc'sle head with Tony. We then helped lower the derricks at #1 then we had chow. After chow I knocked off as I was on the 8-12. On the 8-12 I was shown around the bridge by the 3rd Mate. We passed Breaker Point about 2200. During the day watch I scrubbed out the chartroom, lavatory and entrance of the Bridge and then washed the outside of the wheelhouse down. That night on the 8-12 we started off the watch in mist which by a quarter to nine had gone. We then had a lot of ships mainly in the form of Japanese fishing boats.

Next morning I scrubbed out the wheelhouse and then took the wheel whilst we tested the emergency steering gear. After smoko I sand and canvassed the bridge rails. On Sunday I went on daywork and Dave went on the 8-12. We lowered the lifeboats Monday morning and I was on the motorboat. We arrived in Otaru Monday night about 2330 and anchored outside the breakwater.

Otaru.
17th July 1962 – 20th July 1962.

We were called at 0530 and was supposed to go inside about 0600. We helped the bosun break the cable and at 0800, we finally moved to the buoy. We started cargo immediately. The Mate said two on deck to start off with and then later he changed it to all working and knock off at five. We clean #4 by sweeping up cement dust. In the afternoon I helped the 3rd Mate test the

CO2 fire extinguishers. After that Ike and I wiped up some dirt down #1 and pumped out the wells down there.

On Wednesday I was on cargo in the afternoon with Ike. It was murder trying to keep up with the marks but we managed to do it somehow. I went ashore during the evening and did some shopping and returned on the 11 o'clock launch. It is much cooler now and when we arrived we changed into Blues. Thursday I was on in the evening with Dave, it is easier to keep up with the marks now that are only two hatches, #5 and #2 working. On Friday we sailed at 10 o'clock. I was on the gangway with Ginge and Tony. As we were leaving all the little coasters in the harbour blew their whistles bidding us farewell, almost like the liner *"France"* arriving in New York on her maiden voyage though not quite as spectacular.

Otaru – Hsin Kang.
Friday 20th July – Tuesday 24th July.

As soon as stand-by was over, we began working with the Bosun. We packed the swimming pool away which had just been painted and then after lunch chipped #1 hatch coaming and part of #5. As the Mate is ill I did the last hour of the 4-8 during the evening and the 4-8 in the morning. We passed over Yamato Bank during the last hour and a half of the 4-8. Next day at 0700 we were approaching the straits between Japan and Korea and a sharp lookout was kept for fishing boats. We changed back into whites for breakfast, the weather being very much warmer. During the whole of the trip the visibility kept altering often so that the Captain had to come onto the Bridge.

Sunday I went on to daywork and Monday before breakfast we cleaned out the Bridge. Afterwards we helped the sailors chip #5 and #6 hatch coamings. Tuesday I was called at 0400 to go up for'ard for stand-by. We were anchored about 0430 and then we just had to wait for the search parties. At 0600 a Tug was seen approaching and the pilot ladder was rigged on the starboard side. We had to muster and searches then stand-by went at 0715 and I went up for'ard again. At 8 o'clock David came and relieved me and I went to breakfast. I then went to help with the springs we were alongside by 1000. We then finish cleaning the halfdeck.

Hsin Kang.
Tuesday 24th July – Saturday 28th July.

During the afternoon we cleaned some metal polish off the varnish work on the Bridge. Next day we did the deck head in the halfdeck with flat white. That took all day. So far it has been raining all the time and no cargo has been worked. Thursday the rain stopped and cargo started. Ginge, Dave and I cleaned #1 orlop deck and then we scraped the grey paint on the boat deck. Dave and I put the tent on #3 before lunch. During the afternoon I red leaded the mornings scrapes whilst Ginge and Dave did the after-hand rail on the boat deck. I then red leaded all the scraped handrails and the other two painted the wicker chairs deck head green.

Next morning we chipped and red leaded the bulkhead directly behind the emergency deck controls for the engine room. We sailed Saturday morning at 1000 after the usual musters and inspections I was on the gangway for stand-by and we had it turned in before we left the wharf. The delay was due to a suction dredger dredging across the channel. I then went round locking up the strong rooms and closing the access hatches. We finally left the quay and we put the pilot ladder over on the port side. The Pilot left with the guard about 1150 and we were F.S.A. by 1200. Whilst we were in Hsin Kang we had a lot of rain coupled with high temperatures not a very pleasant state of affairs. Dave and I went ashore one evening and amongst other things bought a Bessy Russian hat each.

Hsin Kang – Kobe.
Saturday 28th July – 31st July.

We had the afternoon off which Ike and I took advantage of and did piles of dhobi in the officers washing machine. We believe that such a machine should be fitted in each halfdeck and then dhobi would be no problem. We also had Sunday off except for the watch keepers who did their normal watches.

I went on the 8-12 and cleaned the bridge up. I scrubbed out the wheelhouse Monday and cleaned odd brass. During the night 8-12, we had about four big lights, two of which I did rising bearings on. Next morning when I went on watch we were just about to anchor. We anchored at 0833. F.W.E. was at 0836. We stayed there until 1654. I was on the foc'sle for stand-by we were all fast at 1817.

Kobe.
Tuesday 31st July – Thursday 9th August.

We were alongside at the Dolphins and we did not work any cargo. We were all on cargo and one on the nights. We worked with the Bosun because the Mate had gone ashore. We did the prom deck rails and the #3 hatch coaming. We red leaded the lot. We had Saturday and Sunday off. On Monday we went alongside. We sailed on Thursday and I was on gangway stand-by.

Kobe – Manila.
Thursday 9th August – Sunday 12th August.

We have been working on the bridge and have sugied the wheelhouse housing and painted the awning spas. The apron has been washed down and partly painted. We had Saturday afternoon off where I did some office work and dhobi. I went on the 12-4 Sunday afternoon and washed down the decks. I then cleaned as much bridge brass as possible. We first sighted land early in the morning but lost it again. At 4 o'clock we had just picked it up again.

We arrived in Manila at about 0415 so I stayed up and did the for'ard stand-by. We anchored and went into the harbour at 0700. There was a lot of vegetation floating about due to the recent floods. We moored in the harbour and I did the 12-4 cargo with Ike. During the night two of us had to be on to keep an eye on the ropes which have a habit of being stolen. We sailed at 1300 on Monday and I was on the bridge and as soon as we were away I changed into working gear and polished brass. It was hot and sunny. During the morning watch the 3rd Mate helped me with some study office work.

On Wednesday morning we sighted Hong Kong at 0200 and from then on there were plenty of ships. At 0400 we only had an hour and a half before the Pilot. I was called at 0700 to stand-by for'ard we were anchored and we were to move to the buoys, ours is "A9". We were all fast at 0840. We unloaded some trans-shipment cargo during the first day and I was on the 12-4 that evening. Some of us went to chow with the Padre at the Missions to Seamen.

Hong Kong.
Wednesday 15th August – Thursday 23rd August.
The following day we worked on the bridge and I painted the radar scanner grey. I went ashore in the evening. On Friday we opened up #3 middle deep tank in the morning and then carried on the bridge. On Saturday we continued with the bridge painting the apron and behind the course boards on the bridge. During the afternoon Dave and I went ashore and did some shopping and then went to the mission again for chow. On Sunday afternoon Dave and I went sailing in the dinghy but there was not really enough wind for a good sail.

On Monday cargo started but I was on day work and painted the radar scanner stand white. On Tuesday we continued on the bridge and in the evening Dave and I went ashore to the China Fleet Club. We, Dave and I, did the 12-6 in the morning but one of us was able to knock off at 0400. Thursday we finally sailed at 1200. The passengers joined at 1030. I was on the gangway and afterwards we washed down and generally tidied up.

Hong Kong – Singapore.
Thursday 23rd August – Monday 27th August.
I was on day work for this trip and it has been a little cooler for the whole trip. On Friday we washed down the paint work on the bridge and the top poop. We then painted the top poop. We had

boat drill at 1615.

Weather is hot and sunny.

We finished off the poop during Saturday morning and had the afternoon off. On Sunday we turned to, to sand and canvas the gangway. Afterwards we had to make 'deck quoits'. We arrived in Singapore at 0745 and anchored in the Eastern Roads.

Singapore.

Monday 27th August – Monday 3rd September.

We unloaded our deck cargo of potatoes and onions in the roads and 1200 we went alongside. I was on gangway stand by. The first evening off I spent aboard. We unloaded hemp from numbers #4, #5 and #6 whilst #3 starboard after deep tank was prepared for latex.

The discharge was finished Wednesday morning and at 1700 we shifted ship one berth astern. The *"Menelaus"* came in at the same time. We filled the starboard after deep tank on Thursday morning and began loading in #2, #4 and #5. We had a big treat Friday morning when the Padre took us to the Tiger Breweries for a tour. In the afternoon I did the 1-5 rather shakily. The next day I was on in the morning and at 1100 it began to rain. During the afternoon Dave and I went swimming.

On Saturday there was a public holiday for the referendum Dave and I again went swimming in the afternoon and then to a dance in the evening. Sunday saw us nearly full but not down to our marks. We have started to load deck cargo on #2 and #4. On Monday we finished and were due to sail at 1500. At 1515 the Pilot was aboard and after a very fast and hairy exit. The Pilot was away at 1600. I was on day work then.

Singapore – Aden via Penang.

Monday 3rd September – Friday 14th September.

The first morning out we discovered that an A.B. had a stone in his kidney and that we will have to put him off. We altered course for Penang and the day jobs included turning out and rigging the gangway and preparing the motor lifeboat for lowering.

The weather is very fine and clear.

The A.B. was taken by the Pilot boat to the hospital and by 1600 we were all full away again.

The trip has nearly all been taken up with washing down and generally kicking our heels waiting for the weather to improve. We washed down the bridge and fiddely on Thursday and I cleaned the sidelights. We were surprised to have the afternoon off for office work. On Friday we cleaned the veranda which was extremely dirty with cigarette ends etc. Then we went on to the bridge brass. We were told that we would have to work the weekend but as the weather has not improved so we only had to Saturday morning.

Sunday was also free so I began my office work to cover my leave. On Monday, Ginge and I went round all of the port boxes in the Mates' alleyway sugiing and painting them. When that was finished, we suggied and distempered the Mates' drying room. On Tuesday Ike and I did the poop ridge wires. We washed down the boat deck bulkheads. On Thursday we were able to start painting as we were in the Gulf of Aden. We washed down the bulwarks.

On Friday we were called at 0430 and I went on the bridge for stand-by. As the R.T. didn't work we missed the first Pilot, so we had to anchor and wait until 0700. When the Pilot arrived we went straight in and were all fast by 0800. At 0830 I went on Deck to watch the starboard fore-cabin and when this was finished I did smoko relief for the centre castle watchers. We then put the plates back into the after end of the centre castle. We went on stand-by at 1145 and I went down aft. We were away at 1345. After lunch we squared up around the decks. Boat drill.

Aden – Suez.
Friday 14th September – Tuesday 18th September.

Ginge and I painted #1 hatch coaming and I did the 1500 – 1600 wheel. All the time now we are painting and Ginger and I kept on with the grey. On Monday afternoon Ginge and I helped the Peggies and Bosun. On Monday evening we arrived in Suez Bay. On the Tuesday morning we entered the canal at 1000.

Suez Canal Transit.
Tuesday 18th September.
Once we were moving Ginge and I dismantled and put away the pool. Then Dave and I began cutting in on the contactor house top. At 1600 we changed Pilots and at 0600 we began to pass the cut. We were clear of Port Said at 2230 and now begins a race for home with the "*Bendoran*[16]". The weather is now much cooler.

Port Said – LIVERPOOL (at last).
Tuesday 18th September – 26th September.
On Wednesday Ginge and I painted #3 hatch coaming and then began the scuppers. On Thursday I had to paint the locking bars silver, this job took all day. On Friday I continued cutting in Grey on the centre castle and then went on to the poop. We had boat drill. Saturday morning was spent cleaning up name plates on the vents and air pipes. We had the afternoon off. Weather is warm, fine and clear.

During the afternoon I did the last of my office work and some dhobi. We had a farewell chow for dinner. Called 0800 and had the day off. No jobs except fans. The day was spent dhobying and discussing the best pastimes for leave.

Called at 0600 Monday and commenced barbarising; after chow Dave went on the 8-12 as we are in fog. I am doing the brass tags on the ship's vent and doors whilst the rest move all the trunks from the after peak. In the afternoon I carried on with the tabs except for a break to shift some cargo in the port fore-cabin.

The "*Benavon*[17]" caught up with us whilst we were reduced in the fog and now we have a race on with her having lost to the "*Bengloe*[18]" and "*Bendoran*" already, this will be the hat trick.

The weather has cleared a little but is still hazy and low swell.

On Tuesday morning we were called at 0600 again and barbarised the prom deck and washed down the for'ard end of the bridge. I finished the tabs before lunch and then began the lifeboat propeller. When this was finished John and I washed down the boat deck. We are now in the Bay of Biscay and there is a moderate sea and some showers.

Wednesday morning before breakfast Ginge, John and I Washed down the fiddely. After I washed down the ladders. During the afternoon we cleaned the halfdeck out. We picked up the Pilot on Thursday morning 0148 we then anchored at the bar until 0715 when we proceeded in. I was on the gangway for stand-by and we were all fast by 0945.

What We Learnt...

This was the first true blue (pun intended) Blue Funnel ship P. J. Wood served on. This trip saw him jaunt around China, Japan the Philippines before swinging back west and through the Suez Canal before arriving back in Blighty, Liverpool to be exact. 323 days since he left the UK as a bright-eyed Midshipman with his Passport and British Seamans card. What were his main duties that were felt important enough to be put into the log? Cleaning the holds, scrapping and painting the ship once again. You could look at this logbook so far, after three voyages and assume that this is just a very extravagant painting and decorating apprenticeship.

I am lucky enough to have a copy of the letter Alfred Holt & Co. sent to Midshipmen in the 1950' and 60's on their appointment and there are very interesting passages of text which set the expectations of any Middy that came joined. One such as below for example:

"The Master of your ship will give you such duties to perform as, in his opinion, will provide you with the best training for the profession of an officer in the Merchant Navy. Every kind of duty will be given you and no such duty must be regarded as beneath your dignity"

They managed to pack the pool away twice in the voyage, obviously putting it up was not worthy of mention, the three times they went shopping were notable enough, this time however, he did come back with a Russian hat. There was a brewery tour (Tiger Brewery in Singapore) with the Padre and four visits to the mission and clubs in around the ports. Other than having to be ever watchful of rope thieves in Manilla the most exciting thing seemed to be the races these ships had going from port to port – and getting the hattrick of beating "Benavon", "Bengloe" and "Bendoran" all of the Ben Line back to Liverpool.

M.V. GLENEARN

November 1962

Master: Radford

"Your business abroad is not to cause resentment and sow discord but to create goodwill and foster understanding between peoples. In this respect you have a unique opportunity to serve not only your country, but the cause of peace in the world."

- *Midshipman Appointment Letter from Alfred Holt & Co. circa 1960*

Voyage of M.V. Glenearn - Map

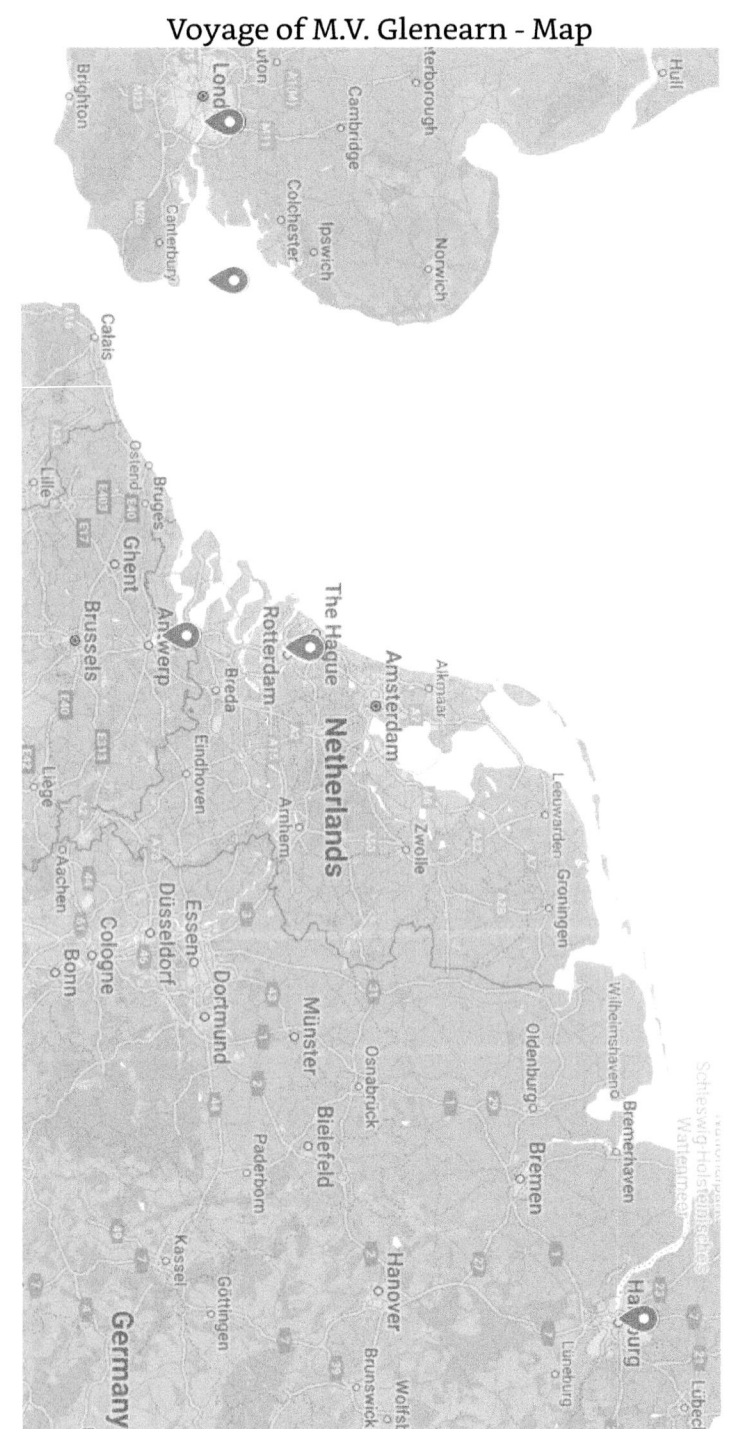

Voyage Statistics

9th November 1962 - London

14th November 1962 - Rotterdam

17th November 1962 - Hamburg

Thursday 29th November 1962 - Antwerp

2nd December 1962 - Rotterdam

Thursday 6th December 1962 - Tongue Lightship

Saturday 8th December 1962 - London

Total number of Ports visited: 6
Total Voyage time: 29 days
Total Voyage Distance*: 1,267 Nautical miles

* All distances are estimated using Reed's New Maritime Distance Tables (1965) [Acquired from Fenton Steamship Co. Chartering and S&P department] and by going "old school" with Lloyds Atlas of World Shipping Ports (30th Edition). Ports, wharfs, jetties and buoys have all changed dramatically over the last 62 years so that calculating accurate distances is nearly impossible to determine, so we used our best judgement.

London.

9th November – 13th November.

We travelled down from Liverpool on the morning train and arrived aboard about 1500. I reported to the Mate who told me that one of us was required for the night, which I did. Steve and I went ashore for a short while in the evening and then returned to the ship to crash. At 0900 Saturday morning I saw Captain Dowey to see if I could go home for the weekend. He kindly gave his permission and by 1000 I was on the bus for Plaistow.

I returned to the ship on Monday morning at 0800 when Steve and I replaced three new halyards, two on the foremast and one on the aftermast. We then cleared out the halfdeck in readiness for the pre-sailing inspection. The inspection was at 1500 and I was on the bridge. This was completed about 1600 and after chow Tony, Steve and I went ashore. I, to meet my mother at Waterloo. We then went to see some friends. I returned to the ship at about 2400. Tuesday was the usual day of blues for us all because we did not have anything to do and were waiting to sail. Stand-by for sailing was at 2115.

London – Rotterdam.

13th November – 14th November.

I was on the poop for stand-by and by the time we had let go at about 2130, I was cold. We were clear of the lock about 2230 and I remained on stand-by aft till about 2315. I then relieved Steve for'ard as he was on the 4-8 and I was on the 12-4, and Tony was on the 8-12. At about 0030 I was able to relieve Tony on the Bridge and I then took up the already fully filled job of lookout. At Southend I sent the ship's name to the shore station. There was an hours clock flog and at 0330 the Pilot left. It was then of course 0430. Next morning at 0815 we were anchored off the Hook of Holland in fog awaiting the departure of the ship that was in our berth. About 1100 we started in. When I went on the Bridge at 1230 we were just approaching the Hook of Holland Ferry berth. At 1400 we were all fast alongside the latex wharves where we just had to discharge the latex.

Rotterdam.
14th November – 16th November.
I was on deck until 1600, when Steve came out, just to keep an eye on developments. At 1830 we shifted ship to a berth about 3 miles upriver and I was on the poop and it was really cold. We were all fast at the new wharf at about 2045 and they were not starting cargo until 2200 and then only with one gang. None of us required that night so we all crashed. Next morning bags of tin ore were discharged from #2 and one of us was required to tally it. This was finished about 1400 and we were supposed to sail at 1700. We did not sail so all three of us went ashore. We arrived back after a pleasant couple of hours ashore at 2200 and we then crashed. Next morning at 0600 the Quartermaster woke us and at 0630 we sailed. I was on for'ard for stand-by and was there all the time until we were clear of the Hook, except for half an hour for breakfast at about 1000. We waited about 20 minutes for the pilot boat and then headed for Hamburg.

Rotterdam – Hamburg.
16th November – 17th November.
When I went on watch at 1230 the visibility was not particularly good and we were almost 'neck and neck' with the *"Polydorus*[19]*"*. By 1600 we were abeam of the minefield off the German coast. I did the chow relief and at 0700 we altered course to 092 degrees. At midnight we were steering at 160 degrees and the *"Polydorus"* was 6 miles astern. The Pilot took over at midnight and at 0145 we were abeam of *"ELBE I Lightvessel*[20]*"*. At 0230 we were abeam of Cuxhaven where we reduced speed for 10 minutes at 0330 we changed Pilots. At 0400 when Steve came up, we were about 2 hours from Hamburg. At 0600 I was called for stand-by and went aft. At 0715 we were all fast.

Hamburg.
17th November.
We unloaded latex here and at 1230 I went on the Bridge and

we shifted ship to a dry cargo berth we were secured about 1330, but at 1430 we moved up the wharf to take the place of another ship. We were all fast again by 1500. We are not working any cargo until Monday morning and we are working the nights, 11-7. I did the night of the 17th. Steve, Tony and I went ashore Sunday afternoon and walked around the centre of Hamburg. We returned to the ship about midnight. Next day cargo started at 7:00 AM and continued until 1500. Monday evening I went ashore again this time with Steve and we went to the Star Club, where several Liverpool groups were performing.

Tuesday morning I tallied some tin and then continued to test the wells and scuppers. We had Wednesday off as it was a national holiday and Tony and I were lucky enough to be able to go on a trip to Lübeck. We were taken with five others in a VW minibus by the Padre of the Mission to Seamen. We saw the Bismarck estates, Bismarck's tomb, on then to Lübeck where we saw two churches which were still under repair from bomb damage. We then went to the East-West border and had an eye-opening time looking at Germans dividing Germany. We returned to the ship via the autobahn and arrived back aboard at 1730 after an extremely enjoyable day.

We shifted into dry dock at 0200 on Thursday morning and we were all fast at 1508. During the day the bottom was scraped and given a coat of paint. 3 cylinders were taken out of the engine room and the anchors were ranged. In the evening, Steve and I went ashore. First thing Friday morning Steve and I helped Chippy put a plug and cover by every vent. I had the afternoon off and went ashore shopping. I'm on the night and it is damn cold inside and out as the heat is off. On Saturday afternoon I went with the 2nd Mate down #9's double bottom to check that enough cement had been put on. Stand-by for moving out of dry dock was at 1500 and I went aft. We were all fast at the Oberhafen Dolphins about 1600. We were moored alongside the "*Fleetbank*[21]". We all stayed aboard and Steve was on the night. The next day, Sunday, we were not called, but I woke up at 10:00 AM and Steve and I went ashore at 1630. On Monday morning,

Steve and I scraped and touched up some spots on the funnel. I had the afternoon off and did the night. At about 1900 we went across to the *"Fleetbank"* and saw the apprentices, then came here and were surprisingly impressed with the halfdeck. Tony went on deck in the afternoon whilst Steve and I went ashore. 25 tons were loaded, mainly into #1 and when on deck at 1830 they had about 20 slings left. This was eventually finished at 2100 and we went on stand-by at 2130.

Hamburg – Antwerp.
Tuesday 27th November 1962 – Thursday 29th November 1962.

I was on the 8-12 and consequently went on the bridge, we ran into fog about 2200. We crept down the river and at 2400 visibility had improved somewhat. When I came on watch at 0830 on Wednesday we had left the Pilot but were still in the buoyed channel. I put her position down every half hour throughout the watch. During the evening watch we passed the entrance to Rotterdam harbour and picked up the Pilot. I was called at 0640 for stand-by and by 0810 we were fast in the locks. After breakfast I went on the Bridge and we were all fast at 1000.

Antwerp.
Thursday 29th November 1962 – Saturday 1st December.

We started cargo immediately to load 1331 tons when I knocked off at 12:30 there were only about 1330 to go. I was on the next morning and we loaded steel in #2 and #3, milk in #1, glass in #5 and asbestos in #4. Tony was given the day off to go to Brussels and managed to leave at 1315. Steve and I were off in the evening and Tony did the night. I was on cargo the following morning and we sailed much to everyone's surprise at 2000. I was on the Bridge stand-by and we had to wait off the locks for 25 hours. We went in at 2300 hours. We were all fast in the locks by 2315 when we were gradually joined by three other ships. At 2400 the lock gates were just opening and I swapped stand-bys with Tony and went on the poop. The ship to the leeward of us left the locks first after smartly bashing us just for'ard of the bridge and breaking one spring.

Antwerp – Rotterdam.
2nd December 1962.
When I came on watch in the morning we had just passed the ferry terminal. We were alongside the wharf by 1000 and we had the rest of the day off. I did the night. Cargo started at 0730 Monday morning.

Rotterdam.
2nd December 1962 – 4th December 1962.
During the afternoon of Monday Steve and I went ashore and found the city very clean. I was on the evening and we loaded into #4 mainly. When I went on again at midday Tuesday we were loading in #1, #2, #3, #4 and #6. Cargo eventually finished at 1630 and we sailed immediately. I was on the bridge and did the 4-8. We were clear of the Hook by 1900 and by 1730 we were in dense fog.

Rotterdam – London.
4th December – Saturday 8th December.
We anchored at about 2000 and when I went on watch in the morning the fog was still dense. At 0800 the Captain decided to continue. We continued all day and when I went on watch in the evening we were near the *"Tongue lightship*[22]*"*. We anchored about 1900.
Thursday morning when I was called we were heaving away. When I arrived on the Bridge we had dropped the anchor again. The whole watch was spent listening to the cockney voice of Gravesend radio telling all ships about all ships. At about 0900 we proceeded again but anchoring in dense fog two hours later. On Friday the weather cleared up and we went up to #17 Barrow. At about 1500 we had instructions to proceed upriver. At 1730 we picked up the Gravesend Pilot and we were off the lock at 2000. We went on stand-by at 2030 and proceeded through the locks, we were all fast by 0300 Saturday.

London.

Saturday 8th December.

At 1000 we had to report to the office to see Captain Dowey when he told us that we could go home until Tuesday night when we should report aboard the *"Glengyle"* for the coasting voyage. We dashed back, paid off, saw the Customs, packed and took our gear across to the *"Glengyle"* and went home. I arrived home at 1434.

What We Learnt…

This coastal voyage toured northern Europe and dealt mainly with supervising the loading and discharging of goods, radio work as well as a fair proportion of sightseeing in the likes of Rotterdam, Lubeck and Hamburg. Which made a change from the scraping and painting of the previous voyages.

The mention of minefields indicates that in 1962 we are not really that far removed from the end of World War II and that the European coast of the North Sea was potentially a very dangerous place to sail. Luckily the only drama mentioned was a minor collision in the locks at Antwerp.

Another birthday onboard ship was achieved, but no sun of the Mediterranean this time. The 18th birthday was spent watching latex being discharged in Rotterdam – the adventure of the sea!

While in Hamburg the sightseeing included visiting the Star Club, which famously hosted the Beatles with their final lineup (now including Ringo instead of Best who had left that August) and would have been part of the "several Liverpool bands were performing" line in the logbook. Timing being everything, they actually had completed their final night three days previously on the 14$^{th\ of}$ November – P. J. Wood I guess was not to gutted about this as he always came across as more a Rolling Stones man.

M.V. GLENGYLE

December 1962

Master:
Mate:
2nd Mate:
3rd Mate:
4th Mate:

<u>Midshipmen</u>

"Omit no opportunity of learning all you can about the stowage of cargo and the problems to be solved if the cargo is to be delivered in a good condition, and preferable in better condition, than when it was loaded."

- *Midshipman Appointment Letter from Alfred Holt & Co. circa 1960*

Voyage of M.V. Glengyle - Map

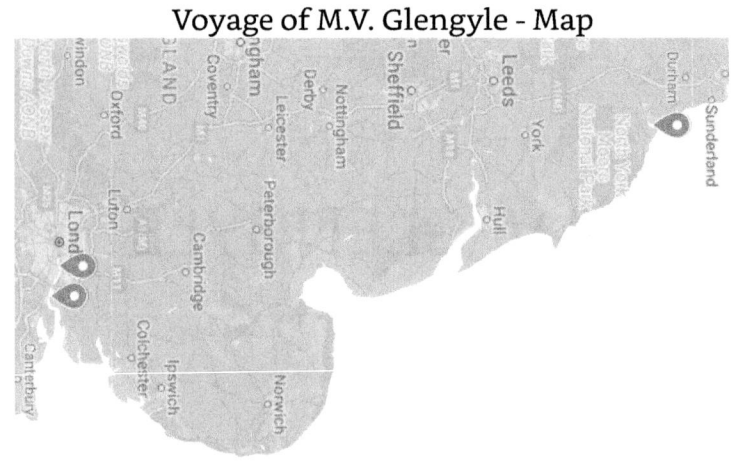

Voyage Statistics

Tuesday 11th December 1962 - London

Thursday 13th December 1962 - Tilbury

Friday 14th December 1962 - Rotterdam

Sunday 16th December 1962 - Hamburg

Wednesday 19th December 1962 - Middlesbrough

Total number of Ports visited: 5
Total Voyage time: 8 days
Total Voyage Distance*: 956 Nautical miles

* All distances are estimated using Reed's New Maritime Distance Tables (1965) [Acquired from Fenton Steamship Co. Chartering and S&P department] and by going "old school" with Lloyds Atlas of World Shipping Ports (30th Edition). Ports, wharfs, jetties and buoys have all changed dramatically over the last 62 years so that calculating accurate distances is nearly impossible to determine, so we used our best judgement.

London.

Tuesday 11th December 1962 – Thursday 13th December 1962.

I arrived back at the dock about 9:15 in the evening with Mother, Janet and Jerry. The police would not allow them through the gate so I dumped my gear, picked up Steve and we all went for a drink. Next day we had the inspection engine trials and signing on. We shifted ship to Tilbury at 2100 and we were there at 2400. We went to the river berth and the night was spent playing about with the ropes. It's a wonder other ships stay alongside the way we have to carry on because of a tide. We sailed on Thursday at midday and I was on the 12-4. We dropped the Pilot at the *"Sunk Lightvessel*[23]*"* at about 1615. Winds increased until about 2200 when we were off the Hook. The pilot service had been suspended and it was not until 0315 that we could pick up a Pilot and moved in. I was called at 0530 to stand-by aft. We were all fast about 0700.

Rotterdam.

Friday 14th December – Saturday 15th December.

We started cargo immediately and worked all through the night. Tin had to be tallied and it was finished about 1:15. We sailed at 4 o'clock in the evening and I was on stand-by aft until 1745.

Rotterdam – Hamburg.

Saturday 15th December 1962 – Sunday 16th December 1962.

The weather was pretty rough when we left the Hook and when I went on watch at 12 o'clock it was about force 8. When I went on watch Sunday lunchtime we had just passed *"Elbe 3*[24]*"*. By 1600 we were off the dock and I went up for'ard for stand-by we were all fast at 1645.

Hamburg.

Sunday 16th December 1962 – Tuesday 18th December 1962.

Steve and I went ashore and Tony did the night. He heard today that he is to go on his M.A.R. course (in Liverpool) one month earlier than expected. On Monday we tested wells and scuppers. I had the afternoon off when I did some shopping. At 0630 on Tuesday we shifted ship to unload another tank of latex. I was on the Bridge for stand-by. We were all fast by 0745. I then rigged some hoses to pressure test the starboard wing tank. We sailed in the evening and I was the 4-8 hence on the Bridge stand-by.

Hamburg – Middlesbrough.
Tuesday 18th December 1962 – Wednesday 19th December 1962.
When I went on watch in the morning we were nearly up to the end of the buoys which mark the northern extremity of the minefields. When I went on watch in the evening we were approaching the Tees entrance. We anchored off to await the Pilot at 1700. We started to move it in at 1800. It was a long slow stand-by and we were not all fast until 2000.

What We Learnt…

This second coastal voyage lasted just 8 days but added ship number 5 to the logbook. Both these coastal voyages lacked any detail of the key crew, which implies a dropping of standards or that they were quite forgettable and by the time he came to write it up he had actually forgotten who he sailed with.

More minefields were mentioned around the German coast and some rough weather (force 8 winds: 30 – 44mph), but as they say, "A smooth sea never made a skilled sailor".

A lot less shopping and sight seeing this voyage and time was taken up with actual seamanship and the supervising of loading latex and tallying tin – which is nice and alliterative and should be used as a title or subtitle at least for some highbrow dissertation on the life and times of midshipmen apprentices on the high seas, which we can all agree by reading the first five chapters, this is unlikely to be unless we really pull out all the stops in the final four.

I'm not holding up much hope, but why don't we find out together by moving onto the M.V. Glenogle.

M.V. GLENOGLE

May 1963
Voy. 2/3 coasting
3 D.S.

Master:	W.J. Moore D.S.C.
Mate:	W.F. Rockett
2nd Mate:	D.H. Clark
3rd Mate:	A.F.J. Diack
4th Mate:	D. Gallagher

Midshipmen

- J. A. Ratcliffe
- W. J. Wilcox
- P. J. Wood
- S. P. Khong
- G. D. Martin
- J. C. Bromfield

"Your course of training during the apprenticeship will offer numerous opportunities to improve your skill, knowledge and ability. Take every opportunity that offers and make the most of them. Studies will be set for you during each voyage and you will be expected to complete theses and return them, together with a report to the Managers, when your vessel returns to this country."

- *Midshipman Appointment Letter from Alfred Holt & Co. circa 1960*

Voyage of M.V. Glenogle - Map

Voyage Statistics

Thursday 23rd May 1963 - London - Joined Ship

Sunday 26th May 1963 - Hamburg

Thursday 30th May 1963 - Rotterdam

Thursday 6th June 1963 - Antwerp

Saturday 8th June 1963 - Middlesbrough

Wednesday 12th June 1963 - Rotterdam

Sunday 16th June 1963 - London

Monday 1st July 1963 - Port Said

Suez Canal Transit

Friday 5th July 1963 - Aden

Saturday 13th July 1963 - Singapore

Thursday 18th July 1963 - Bangkok

Thursday 25th July 1963 - Hong Kong

Tuesday 30th July 1963 - Tsingtao

Friday 2nd August 1963 - Yokohama

Thursday 8th August 1963 - Shimizu

Friday 9th August 1963 - Nagoya

Saturday 10th August 1963 - Kobe

Friday 16th August 1963 - Hong Kong

Thursday 22nd August 1963 - Singapore

Monday 26th August 1963 - Port Swettenham (Port Klang)

Friday 30th August 1963 - Penang

Thursday 5th September 1963 - Aden

Sunday 8th September 1963 - Suez Bay

Suez Canal Transit

Monday 9th September 1963 - Port Said

Tuesday 17th September 1963 - London

Total number of Ports visited: 25
Total Voyage time: 117 days
Total Voyage Distance*: 26,891 Nautical miles

* All distances are estimated using Reed's New Maritime Distance Tables (1965) [Acquired from Fenton Steamship Co. Chartering and S&P department] and by going "old school" with Lloyds Atlas of World Shipping Ports (30th Edition). Ports, wharfs, jetties and buoys have all changed dramatically over the last 62 years so that calculating accurate distances is nearly impossible to determine, so we used our best judgement.

London, 1963.
Thursday 23rd May – Saturday 25th May.

I joined the ship at about 1500 and I was settled in by 1700. There are three other Middies on the coast and they stayed from the deep-sea voyage. Friday was spent standing by in the halfdeck mainly and in the evening the other three started watches. We sailed at 0100.

London – Hamburg.
Saturday 25th May – Sunday 26th May.

I was on the foc'sle for stand-by and by 0300 we were clear of the locks and I relieve George on the poop. I was down there until 0445 when I crashed. I was called again at 0700 for the pilot ladder and after that I cleaned out the halfdeck. We picked up the Pilot at about 2230 and from then until stand-by chow at about 0400 I was in and out of my wagon. For stand-by I was on gangway. We were alongside 0515.

Hamburg.
Sunday 26th May – Tuesday 28th May.

I was called again for shifting ship at 0930 and stand-by went about 1030. I was on the poop for stand-by and we were alongside Kaiser Wilhelm [Kaiser-Wilhelm-Höft] about 1145. We continued unloading with one on and one on daywork until Monday 27th. The day worker, me, did a few wells and scuppers.

Hamburg – Rotterdam.
Tuesday 28th May – Wednesday 29th May.

Stand-by was at 0900 and I was on the gangway. It was a lovely day and the whole of the country looked inviting. I was required for the pilot ladder at odd intervals and in-between times were spent clearing out the halfdeck. Just before the Pilot was due to leave we ran into fog. The Pilot eventually left at 1700. We proceeded in fog until we arrived at Rotterdam 24 hours later. After picking up the Rotterdam Pilot and proceeded in we left the fog behind us and we went alongside the latex wharf at about 1600. After unloading the last tank we shifted ship to the dry cargo berth. I was for'ard for stand-by and we were all fast by 0100.

Rotterdam.
Thursday 30th May – Wednesday 5th June.
When all the cargo was finished we move to the Wilton drydock but not before we had tested the remaining wells and scuppers and having removed some rather unpleasant intestine like mess from #5 A.P. well. We shifted ship to the drydock Friday morning when I was aft for stand-by. Stand-by was at 0715 and we were all fast by 0845. The dock (floating) was dry by 1000 and the hull was begun by sandblasting. The prop was to be tested so I went off to warn people to keep clear but this was over in half an hour. The drill in drydock was 3 on day work and 1 on night. I did Saturday night. Sunday afternoon, Adam, George, three engineers and I went to the beach at Scheveningen and had an extremely entertaining afternoon. Monday, being Whit Monday was also free, but as we had no money, we just sat around lapping up the sun. Tuesday was spent just sitting around "standing-by", and Wednesday we were due to sail in the afternoon. We eventually sailed at 10 o'clock and the Pilot was away at midnight.

Rotterdam – Antwerp.
Thursday 6th June.
When I went on watch the next morning we were well up the river and at 0930 we anchored off the locks. After a lot of false alarms, we heaved up the anchor at 1215. We were in locks for quite a while and I was on stand-by aft, we were eventually all fast by 1500.

Antwerp.
Thursday 6th June – Friday 7th June.
Stand-by the leaving was at 1400 and by 1430 we were anchored off the locks again. This time I was for'ard. We were in the locks by 1800 and we left them about 1845. At midnight the Pilot was away.

Antwerp – Middlesbrough.
Friday 7th June – Saturday 8th June.

We ran into fog about 0400 and when I went on watch we were on stand-by full speed. By 1100 it had cleared up enough to increase speed. At about 1400 we anchored. At 1530 we weighed anchor and for stand-by I was on gangway. We were all fast by 1730.

Middlesbrough.
Saturday 8th June – Tuesday 11th June.

There was just one Middy required for the night. So Adam, George and I went to a dance. I was on cargo Sunday morning and I spent a soul destroying 6 hours watching cargo. I went on to daywork Monday and helped Chippy with a few jobs. On Tuesday, I spent the morning trying to get the rust stains off the deck around the two aft winches on the wooden decks. We sailed at 1530 and I was for'ard for stand-by. We spent about one and half hours off the river calibrating the D.F. and then the Pilot was away at about 2000.

Middlesbrough – Rotterdam.
Tuesday 11th June – Wednesday 12th June.

Again we ran into fog fairly quickly and we did not arrive in Rotterdam until midday. I was for'ard for stand-by and we were all fast by 1500.

Rotterdam.
Wednesday 12th June – Saturday 15th June.

We worked cargo until 0230 Thursday morning and started again at 0600. I was still on daywork and I was removing paint splats from the rusty deck. In the afternoon I did some shopping for the Mate. Friday it rained all day until about 1600 and no cargo was worked until then. Saturday morning I helped Chippy with some trimming off. We sailed at 1600 I was on the gangway and the Pilot was away at 1830.

Rotterdam – London.

Saturday 15th June – Sunday 16th June.

We had clear weather all the way across with winds about force 5. We arrived at Gravesend as 0330, and I was called at 0230 for the Pilot gear. At 4:15 we were swinging off the locks and we went in immediately. I was on the foc'sle for stand-by. We were alongside by 0515.

London.
Sunday 16th June – Tuesday 25th June.

Mother at the helm

At 0830 we were told that I was to stand-by until she sailed and the others were to go home. I was on the night and I was allowed to go home immediately. I arrived back at the ship at 2300 and did the night. Nothing eventful happened. At 0645 Adam Slater left to catch the 0715 train. John Bromfield and Jim Wilcox were to join imminently so the Mate said I could go home and return the following morning. On my return I showed John around the ship and did a couple of messages for the Mate and at lunchtime returned home to return that night for the night.

I did Tuesday and Wednesday night and returned Friday morning again. I did Saturday night and the deep-sea Mate, Mr Rockett joined. I went home Saturday with instructions to return Sunday morning, which I did. Only to return home in less than an hour.

That afternoon I showed my mother around the ship and we went home together. I returned to the ship Monday morning. We were due to sail at 1430 but couldn't finish the cargo, so we sailed at 0230 Tuesday.

London – Port Said.
Tuesday 25th June (a.m.) – Monday 1st July (p.m.)

I was on the gangway but when we cleared the locks at 0400 I crashed for the 8-12. When I went on the bridge at 0830 we were just about to pass the *"S. Goodwin Lt. ship*[25]*"*. At 0845 we passed Dover harbour and at 0930 we dropped the Pilot at Dungeness. There was a mist and a miserable wind. At about 1100 we passed the *"Royal Sovereign Lt. ship*[26]*"*. When I went on watch in the evening we were near Ushant which we passed about 2200. We put the clocks back an hour to GMT at Midnight.

Wednesday saw us in the bay [Bay of Biscay] with mist and moderate swell. We rounded Finisterre in the evening 8-12. Thursday morning. We round St. Vincent and the weather was notably warmer. At 2000 that evening we were abeam of Gibraltar and by midnight we were 90 miles into the Mediterranean.

Friday morning we went into whites. The weather is much better and the temperature is above 70 degrees Fahrenheit. During the Friday evening 8-12 we passed Cap Serrat. Saturday morning there was a 45-minute clock flog. We were in bearings Saturday morning and we were approaching Pantelleria. The air conditioning is now on and outside certainly feels extremely humid by comparison. Jim, Giles and John put the swimming pool up this morning and during the afternoon we made a few deck cricket balls.

Saturday evening was my last 8-12 for this week. We were between Sicily and Malta when I went on watch and at 2130 we left that land. The weather is much warmer and I certainly do appreciate the air conditioning. Sunday morning Khong and

Johnny put up the deck cricket net on the aft deck. During the rest of the day was spent doing office work, dhobying and sunbathing.

Monday morning we were called at 0530 and turn to at 0600. John and I turned to with the crew overhauling the gear until breakfast. After breakfast John and I helped the Chippies do the derrick heels whilst Khong carried on with the crew overhauling the gear aft. At 1630 we went on stand-by for anchoring. I went for'ard and four shackles were put in the water.

Port Said.
Canal transit.
Tuesday 2nd July.

We went on stand-by at 0130 and Kong and I were for'ard. Port Said looked and smelt just the same as it did 9 months ago. We were moored to the buoys at 0245 and the watch keepers stayed on watch for the 217 bags of mail that we unloaded and the potatoes which we were to load. At 0725 we were called again to go on stand-by immediately I was on gangway and this was finished by 0800 and we entered the canal number 4 in the convoy of 10 ships. The Mate said we could have the morning off, which was spent mainly replying to letters received in Port Said. At 1105 we went on stand-by to moor in the cut Kong and I were for'ard again. We were all fast by 1145. During the afternoon we stood by in the halfdeck. The temperature rose to 98 degrees Fahrenheit in the shade outside. But it was cool 73 degrees inside. 10 tankers and 15 cargo ships, including *"Ixion*[27]*"* passed in the northbound convoy and we went on stand-by at 1700 to leave the cut. We are all clear by 1725 we entered the Bitter Lakes at about 1830. John stayed up to do the gangway and we were clear off the canal by 2350. F.S.A. was at 2400.

Suez – Aden.
Wednesday 3rd July (a.m.) – Friday 5th July (p.m.)

Called at 0530 and turn to at 0600 to scrub the lifeboat oars and boathooks. After breakfast we stacked all the stores ready for checking. When the oars were dry we linseed oiled them. We then put some new lashings on the for'ard and aft ends of the boat cover. After lunch we started to check the stores by replacing the condensed milk, 109 tins for each boat. #1 boats fuel tank had leaked and I had to hold a bucket underneath the plug by standing on the trestle from the boat deck. After smoko we finished packing the stores and replaced the oars.

Thursday we turned to before breakfast Khong in the halfdeck and John and I scraping all the varnish in the lifeboats. After breakfast John and Khong carried on with scraping and I helped Chippy overhaul the McGregor hatch blocks. We did one and half hatches before lunch and in the really sweltering heat. After lunch Khong helped Chippy and John and I continued in the boat. The temperature reached 103 degrees Fahrenheit in the shade where we were working. We had boat drill at 1615 and Engine Room fire drill.

Friday we turned to at 0600, again scraping varnish in the lifeboats. After lunch we Turned to for about half an hour before we went on stand-by. Giles and I went for'ard and it was certainly a long and hot stand-by. We were all fast for'ard at 1500 but they weren't fast aft until about 1520. The "*Autolycus*[28]" was just astern of us when we arrived.

Aden
Friday 5th July.
Whilst we were there one was required to help Chippy whilst the rest of us were off. We spent a couple of hours bargaining for radios, projectors, flip flops, tape recorders, films and cigarettes behind the safe barrier of 'no money'. We were called at 2345 and went on stand-by at midnight. No soon as we were clear we started to put the ropes away. We finished stand-by at 0145. F.S.A. was the same time.

Aden – Singapore.
Saturday 6th July – Saturday 13th July.
Called at 0530 and turned to at 0600 to carry on scraping the

lifeboats. This is a very long job and will take about another week I should think. The weather has worsened now to the S.W. monsoon. We are rolling quite a bit now so what will it be like out of the lee of Socotra. I went on the 12-4 at midnight and we were rolling heavily. We passed the "*Flintshire*[29]" at 0015 and by 0200 the wind had moderated to force 4. I did 'rounds' at 0200 and fire patrol at 0300. John was on the 4-8 and when he came up we had just altered course to 105 degrees and the rolling started again. John, the first tripper is fairly seasick and can't eat. Nothing eventful happened Sunday afternoon, the wind is back to force 7. The 2nd Mate gave me from 2-3 off which was much appreciated.

Monday mornings 12-4 was 15 minutes shorter thank goodness. The weather has moderated a great deal but no stars were visible. At noon we were 464 miles from Minicoy [Island] and during the 12-4, we didn't see one ship.

Tuesday morning the clocks were advanced another 30 minutes and the watch was thankfully 15 minutes shorter. My average of two bawling outs a watch has still not been ruined. We didn't pass one ship. We were abeam of Minicoy at 1130 and noon was on bearings. The afternoon watch went uneventfully but we did pass a ship going the other way. The others are still scraping the lifeboat varnish, but they have completed one boat and now on to the next.

Wednesday morning we sighted one ship and I just kept a lookout, did an error and the 4 o'clock R. B. At 0730 the first radar bearing was taken of Ceylon [Sri Lanka] and the departure was at 1230. During the afternoon, we sighted 6 ships. The day workers have linseed oiled one boats boards.

Thursday mornings watch went very quickly because it took about one and half hours to get my error correct. 39 minutes were put on the clocks. One ship again. During the afternoon three ships were graced by our close monitoring and my sight. Error and D.R. worked out satisfactorily.

Friday morning we altered course off Pulo Weh [Pulau We] there was quite a bit of rain about at first this voyage since we left the channel. During the afternoon we passed quite a few ships including the '*Glenroy*' bound for Port Swettenham.

Saturday morning we had an alter course and about 10 ships. The weather has been showery with bright intervals winds about force 3. We were approaching Singapore during the 8-12 and when I went on watch Saturday afternoon we are in the Eastern Roads waiting to go in after a French ship. We were eventually alongside at 1318.

Singapore.
Saturday 13th July – Tuesday 16th July.

I went on cargo immediately. There were nine gangs. Cars were unloaded from #3, #5 and #6. My job to start off with was to drive the cars onto the slings. When they were finished, Khong and I took it in turns to watch the spirits down in #3. The Mate wants two Middy's on the during the day and evening and a Middy on the night. I was off Saturday evening and I visited Steve Jones and Sean O'Mahoney on the "*Stentor*[30]". I returned aboard about 2330.

I was on the following morning, Sunday and during the afternoon John and I went to Changi beach. It was really fabulous and we both enjoyed the trip very much. Sunday evenings watch was spent watching cargo in #3. Monday morning John and I went ashore shopping and sightseeing again. We took plenty of photos and the weather was very hot. In the afternoon we watched cargo down #3. This sort of job is absolutely boring, cannot be done efficiently and is soul destroying. In fact, it should be left to the men who are paid to be bored. During the evening John and I went to Connell House and had a game of billiards. We both worked Tuesday morning and as soon as cargo finished we rushed ashore to do some more sightseeing. We went to St. Andrews Cathedral and afterwards saw a snake charmer and took photos of each other with snakes around our necks. We returned aboard about 1445 and we went on stand-by at 1700. John and I were aft and had a very energetic but enjoyable stand-by. We filtered through all the ships in the

Western Roads. F.S.A. was at 1800.

Singapore – Bangkok via Singapore.
Tuesday 16th July – Thursday 18th July.
After the chow the Mate sent for me and when I saw him, he told me to 'dog' all the watertight doors. I had done the aft ones when I was walking for'ard and I passed a bloke standing by the port gangway. When I had past him, I thought it was strange place for a passenger to stand. I went back and asked him if he was a passenger to which he said no. I then asked him what he was doing on board and he replied that he had no right to be here. I asked him if he was a stowaway in an interrogative statement which he confirmed. I told him he'd better come and see the Mate and showed him to the bridge. Here the Mate asked him where he was from and at first he said he was on a ship called the "*Lucia*[31]" and said it was a Blue Funnel Ship. The Mate called the purser and told the fellow to answer correctly to his questions. He then told us that he was off "*HMS Lion*[32]". I then continued with the watertight doors and afterwards helped to 'stand guard' over him in the 5th Mates room. We had by this time turned around and by 2015 we were approaching Singapore Roads again. The immigration came out and took him ashore and we headed for Bangkok again.

Wednesday Morning Khong, John and I were called at 0530 and I saw the Mate who told me to wash the bulkheads on the Prom' deck and after breakfast put the transmitter in the lifeboat as emergency boat drill would be at 1000. All of us except Johnny went in the boat and there was quite a heavy swell running. We tested the transmitter and did some pulling and then returned to the ship. We were away again by 1030. We then continued with the Prom' deck and nearly finished it before lunch. After lunch we finished the Prom' deck and put the covers back on the boats and then did some office work.

Before breakfast on Tuesday, Khong and I undid all of the claws on the McGregor hatches and then Sand and canvassed the teak wood rails around the lifeboats. We passed Cape Liant about

0730. The weather is sunny wind force 2/3. After breakfast we took the covers off the auxiliary steering gear on the poop preparatory to testing it. All of us except John who is on the 8-12 were down there and we eventually had to do the inevitable pumping. This was finished before smoko and then Khong and I went round all of the scuppers and lavatories in the ship putting disinfectant down them. We anchored off Bangkok bar at 1151. I was for'ard for stand-by which was over about 1215. I got the <u>density</u> for the 4th Mate and put a ladder over the stern so he could read the draft. After lunch, Khong, John and I scraped the varnish off the box covering, the sounding gear, the ensign box and a grating.

Bangkok.
Thursday 18th July – Sunday 21st July.
We put another coat of linseed oil on the poop varnish and on Friday we finished off down there. During the morning we all had a go on the sounding machine. In the afternoon we scraped the smoke helmet box and put one coat of linseed oil on it and then knocked off. Stand-by for leaving the anchorage went at 1645 and by 1655 we had made a lee for the Pilot and he was aboard.

At Paknam the immigration came aboard and Johnny did the gangway stand-by for going alongside at 1930 and we were all fast by 2030. Went on sixes for watching cargo and one on deck. We watched down #3 and #5 a job not even the laziest among us could work up the enthusiasm for. Johnny, John and I did from 9 until 12 and from then on the 6-12 until we sailed Sunday afternoon. Saturday afternoon, the three of us went on a tour of the temples in which we saw the White Marble temple, the standing Buddhas 100 foot high, the main temple where there is a standing Buddha 160 foot long (The largest in Thailand) and a solid gold Buddha weighing five and half tonnes. (A craven image?).

Sunday morning One of us was knocked off so we all had a long smoko. Cargo finished at about 1500 and we tested gear at

1532. We were clear of the wharf at 1630 and I am on the 4-8. I was on the bridge. I kept her going on the chart and when Khong relieved me for chow we had nearly reached the Pilot vessel. At 1900 the Pilot was away and we then steamed for half an hour to get well clear and then we stopped to have some repairs done on the main engines. We stopped at 1942 this job which was to have taken half an hour took until 2230 when F.S.A. was rung.

Bangkok – Hong Kong.
Sunday 21st July – Thursday 25th July.

Monday morning when I went on watch, nothing was doing. I called the day workers at 0530 and after I had changed, I did the humidity. Later I took an <u>error</u>. The weather has been showery, wind about force 3. In the evening 4-8 we were on bearings and at 1830 altered course off Pulo Payung. We altered course again at 1948 off Pulo Obi. I did the usual humidity. At 2315 we altered course again 071 degrees. When I went on watch the next morning it was still dark. I called the day workers at 0530. After I had changed, I did the humidity and took a sight. We arrived in Hong Kong at approximately 0100 Thursday morning. The Old Man took us into the quarantine anchorage to await the Pilot and immigration. We went alongside at 0715 and were all fast at 0805. I was on the bridge.

Hong Kong.
Thursday 25th July 1963 – Saturday 27th July 1963.

We went onto sixes immediately, one watching down #3 and one down #5 with one on deck. John, Khong and I were off until 1230. #5 wasn't open when we went on, so two on deck and one down #3. By 1530 all the spirits were unloaded from #3 and we then I had to watch cigarettes down there. Most annoying when the strongroom was half full with condensed milk.

I went ashore in the evening with John to do some shopping and we met John Wilson and Ginge Hargreaves off the "*Laomedon*[33]". We were on next afternoon again and this time we watched about 10 cartons of cigarettes down #3 and ice cream in #4. The chicken essence having finished in #5. That evening I went on again at 2000 so that Jimmy could go ashore, I spent the first hour down #3 cursing the stupidity of someone who had put ciggies down there when the strongroom was half empty. Taff, Khong and I were on next morning and again we watch down #3 whilst two of us did wells and scuppers. Taff and I went ashore at 1300 to do some last-minute shopping. We returned aboard at 1500 and we sailed at 1800. I was on the bridge for stand-by and the Pilot was away at 1830. I finished off the 4-8 and when Taff relieved me at 2000 we were about 20 sails insight.

Hong Kong – Tsingtao.
Saturday 27th July – Monday 29th July.
I was on daywork Sunday and we were called at 0630 to clean the halfdeck. After breakfast we turned to testing wells in #4. This was finished at 10:15 and we had the rest of the day off.

Monday we were called at 0530 and shifted cargo away from #5 D.T. expansion tanks, after that we unlocked all the access doors and removed the boat covers. After breakfast we washed the bulkheads, scraped the doors and scrubbed the deck of the Tally clerk's office. We were given the afternoon off for office work. We were called at 2400 and went to the muster when this was over we crashed again but for only about half an hour I was on poop stand-by, and after a lot of mucking about we were alongside by 0245.

Tsingtao.
Tuesday 30th July – Thursday 1st August 1963.
The muster started immediately and we walked past the commissar about 0310. We sat down in the lounge and then waited for the searches to end. At 0410 it was over. For a pleasant change the Mate only wanted two on and Johnny and I are doing the 8-12. Rain prevented them from starting cargo until 1020, but the intervening time was spent testing wells and scuppers. When they did start loading it was in the U.T.D. starboard fridge

locker. Our job was to supervise and the use of egg sticks in stow. The first decent cargo job we've had since the ship hit the coast. During the evening they commenced loading in the L.H. where I spent two hours unrelieved. Johnny was putting coins in a stow of barrels.

Wednesday morning, it rained again this time until 0920. When the rain did stop, a lot of time was wasted rigging a Derek over the coaster alongside. They started eventually about 1115. When we went on watch in the evening they had started #5 loading but this stopped for no apparent reason at 1000. At midnight when we finished the L.H. was about two-thirds full.

Thursday, August 1st is Little Wendy's first birthday. At 0830 the L.H. was just being covered and L.T.D. port after lockers was to start. #5 loaded two descending slings and then stopped and the gang then went to #1 to load wet pig skins in the starboard fore cabin. After putting a little dunnage in they stopped work there and eventually at 1130 they began loading them at a great rate of bales. When Khong relieved me at 1230 they had about half finished. Smelling a bit high I took flight to the halfdeck and had a good shower and dhobyed my working gear. When I went on watch in the evening we only had 50 bags of groundnuts and 50 bales of cotton waste blankets to load and this was finished by 2115. The muster began at 2200 and we went on stand-by at 2315. I was for'ard for stand-by and with John and after helping the Chippy to close #5, we closed and dogged all watertight doors. The Pilot was away about 0030.

Tsingtao – Yokohama.
Friday 2nd August – Sunday 4th August.
We were called at 0630 Friday to clean out the room before breakfast. After breakfast, Johnny and I moved the aft tier of cargo from the wings of #6 and restowed them on the for'ard side so that the surveyor will be able to check the #7 D.T. We then stacked all the old dunnage on the square so it can be removed in 'Yoko'. When this was finished, we collected and stacked all of the old dunnage in #3. We had boat and fire drill at 1615, after

which we played cricket.

Saturday we were called as usual and we had to scrub the boat covers. Before breakfast we did one and after we put it back and scrubbed the other. The second wasn't dry until 1315 when we then lashed it properly. We had the afternoon off and I caught up on some sleep but I can't remember when it had past me. At midnight Saturday we changed watches and I am to go on the 8-12. Sunday morning. When I went on watch we were already anchored in Yokohama quarantine anchorage.

Yokohama.
Sunday 4th August – Wednesday 7th August.

We waited for the quarantine to come out and eventually at 0930 they arrived bringing with them excrement test gear which put rather a cloud over the ship. Eventually, though, we only had to muster to prove we didn't have cholera. 'Q' was taken down at 1030 and then we simply waited for a Pilot. One arrived at 1245 and we moved in at 1300. I was on the wires aft for stand-by. We were alongside by 1415. We did not work cargo that day until 0800 Monday morning. During the evening. Taff, Johnny and I went ashore.

Monday I wasn't on until the evening, so I went to Tokyo with the Doc. We left about 1030 and arrived in Tokyo at 1140. We had a very good day visiting the Kodokan, International Judo Headquarters and the Tokyo Tower and the area of 'million' bars. We returned to the ship about 1700. I was on with Johnny during the evening and we tested #5 for'ard scuppers, #2 for'ard D.T. Wells, fore cabin scuppers, strongroom scuppers and all the CO_2.

Tuesday I was raked out of bed at 1000 to go with John and Khong to Kamakura and Enoshima. We left the ship at 1030 and went to Yokohama Central Station and boarded a train for Kita Kamakura. Here we got off and spent about three quarters of an hour in a rather uninteresting temple. We then walked onto another large temple where we thought we'd find Daibutsu (Large Buddha). We asked a young couple which way to go and they told us it wasn't there, but we could follow them to it. We went by taxi to Daibutsu and then went by bus with them to a seaside resort called Enoshima. Here we had a very nice time and we had lunch with them. Octopus, two types of fish and seaweed. Okay when you're hungry. We then went through some caves and returned to the station footsore and weary about 1630. We reached Yokohama about 1720. Where we said 'sayonara' and we were aboard by 1740. John and I were on during the evening watching mail in #7 and one on deck.

Wednesday, I turned to at 0600 watching mail at #7 and at 0730 the tanks were inspected and the cleaning gangs then cleared up their stages etc. John relieved me for chow and I then went on deck. No cargo started until 1000 although the gangs were on board and I then went down to the strong room for a few specials to be loaded. John, Giles and Taff were supposed to be going on a picnic but the coach didn't pick them up so during the afternoon they went to Enoshima. Khong, Johnny and I worked the 12-6 between us. John and I had the evening off until we sailed at 2300.

Yokohama – Shimizu.
Wednesday 7th August – Thursday 8th August.

I was on the bridge for stand-by and we were clear of the breakwaters at 2330 and when John relieved me at midnight we were almost clear of the Bay. F.S.A. was at 0012. We arrived in Shimizu at 0515 and we anchored to await the Pilot. When I went on the bridge, a small boat was approaching which turned out to be the pilot boat. We commenced weighing anchor at 0850 and at 0900 the anchor was away. We were alongside at 1000. We started cargo about 1020 with one gang. First we had 180 cartoons of fridge cargo, then 540 cartons in the #4 U.T.D. Just as they started to load this they knocked off for chow. Cargo finished at 1600 and we sailed at 1700. I was on the gangway. We dropped the Pilot at 1720.

Shimizu – Nagoya.

Thursday 8th August.

There is a typhoon in the vicinity and there is a terrific swell and we are pitching easily. The sky is overcast and during the whole 8-12 we could not get an error. At about 2215 we altered course and had about quarter of an hour's violent rolling, but we were soon in the lee of Nagoya Bay. We were soon completely in the Bay and at 2351 we anchored, not knowing when we would go in because of the typhoon.

Nagoya.
Friday 9th August.

I was called at 0600 to stand-by for'ard and with quite a strong wind but sunny morning we were alongside by 0730. I went on deck at 0830 and we immediately loaded a little bit of fridge cargo. We then shifted to #4 U.T.D. The weather was getting worse all the time and it looked as though we would have to shift to the bay again until the typhoon passed. At 1600 though cargo was finished and at 1700 we sailed. I was on the poop for stand-by.

Nagoya – Kobe.
Friday 9th August – Saturday 10th August.

When I went on watch at 2000, we were just about clear of the narrows at the entrance to the bay. When we were clear of the bay we started to pitch more and more until at 2151 we reduced speed to 14 knots this was alright until 2315 when we had to reduce again, this time to 12 knots. When I crashed she was still taking the sea alright. We altered course about 0300 Saturday morning and we started rolling. We anchored off Kobe to await the Pilot at 0700. The trouble was about 50 ships had done the same because of the typhoon. We spent a frustrating 4 hours on the bridge watching pilot boats go to about 40 other ships. Stand-by for going alongside about 1320. I was for'ard for stand-by. We were all fast by 1430.

Kobe.
Saturday 10th August – Tuesday 13th August.

John and I were on deck during the afternoon, one down #7 watching mail and the other having walk around. The 3 D.T.'s were being filled at the same time in preparation for pressure test on Sunday. Cargo finished about 1700 and one still stood by whilst the chippies screwed down the manhole covers. John and I went ashore during the evening.

I was called at 0715 Sunday for 0730 breakfast and when we went on deck at 0810 no cargo was being worked but we shifted 177 bags of mail from #7 to #6. We then had to clear the deck in the Chippies shop in preparation for the D.T. surveyor. When we had knocked off at 1230 no cargo had been worked. During the evening #4 and #3 started discharging in earnest and when John and I went on at midnight, they had just started to scrape in the aft end of #3 L.H. The fridge cargo was coming out very quickly from #4.

During Wednesday morning, the sheet of scrap was dropped and cracked a beam on the tank top. During Wednesday afternoon we had a difficult job making the gangs put the cargo where it was wanted and it was really quite a fruitless task. Cargo finished at 1500 and we sailed at 1600. I was on the poop with John. We had finished by 1640.

Kobe – Hong Kong.
Tuesday 13th August – Friday 16th August.

During the evening we just read and wrote letters. We were called at 0530 Wednesday and put more sand in the cigarette boxes on the prom deck. We then shifted the cargo in #6, which we moved between Tsingtao and Yokohama, to its original position. After that we went to #5 and stacked all the dunnage in the U.T.D. making a sling of the dirty and useless stuff. After lunch we lay dunnage in the aft end of #3 L.H. putting flat on 3x3 probably because of the cracked seam on the tank top. We then painted all the port boxes in the halfdeck.

Thursday we turned to at 0600 with the bosun holy stoning the bridge and boat decks. After breakfast we sugied and scraped the starboard winch on the engineer's deck. During the afternoon we did part of the port winch and the engine room hatch. We had boat drill and engine room fire drill at 1615 and we discharged a powder type fire extinguisher which took me about an hour to refill.

Friday morning Johnny and I carried on with the winches on the Engineers deck. S.B.E. for entering Hong Kong was 1221. Stand-by went for anchoring at 1238. We anchored for about 10 minutes for immigration and then we moved to our buoy A16. We watched the sailors and chippy break the cable and then we're all fast at about 1430.

Hong Kong.
Friday 16th August – Monday 19th August.
Johnny and I were on deck until 1830 as the Mate only wants two on all the time. We didn't have much to do as cargo didn't start until 1800. We did remove some broken glass from the veranda window and watched some D.T. lids being taken off. When Khong and John took over cargo was just about starting. John, Taff and I went ashore during the evening and we did quite a bit of shopping.

When we went on watch Saturday morning we had to watch down #1 and #3. During the afternoon John and I went to shore and I bought a radio. Sunday mornings 12-6 was quite quiet with one on deck and one down #3. Sunday afternoon Johnny, Khong, John and I went on a launch picnic with the Mission. There were quite a few other chaps and we went to picnic bay and anchored for a swim and then went back via "*Aberdean*[34]". Khong and I were on during the evening and I tallied mail for about the first hour. We sailed Monday morning about 0700 but I was not needed for stand-by.

Hong Kong – Singapore.
Monday 19th August - Thursday 22nd August.
I was on the 12-4 and when I went up at 1230 we were not on bearings and we were steering 182 degrees. Nothing happened all watch and I noted that the flying fish of the China Sea are

much bigger and fly further than those of the of the Indian Ocean. During the morning watch I just took an error and the clocks were retarded 60 minutes. Tuesday afternoon the wind picked up quite a bit and noon was 1337. The altitude being about 89 degrees. Wednesday morning the clocks were retarded 30 minutes and will be the last flog until the Indian Ocean.

Taff, Giles and John are on day work and they have been Scraping, red and pink leading the winches and hatches on the aft end of the engineer's deck. When I went on watch Thursday morning, we were on bearings and at 0100 the Old Man came up and stayed up until we had anchored at 0406. We moved to alongside at 0715 and I was called to go aft just before we were alongside. We were all fast by 0830.

Singapore.
Thursday 22nd August – Sunday 25th August.
Sixes again, Khong and Giles are going home and the Mate wants two on. One watching down #3 and one down #1. What a very good training. Johnny and I are on during the afternoon and Jock Martin came around in the morning from the *"Agapenor"*. We unloaded mainly during the 1-5 in the afternoon. That evening Jock and I went to shore together and as they weren't working cargo during the morning 1-5, I did the 3-6.

At 0430 I called the Third Mate and at 0500 everyone else was called for shifting ship. Gear was tested at 0530 and 0600 standby went. We were only shifting one go down ahead and I was on the gangway. We were all fast again at 0715 and I crashed. Still watching when I went on at 1230 and at 1700 the *"Agapenor"*, which was ahead of us, sailed. Cargo was worked 1-5 on the second half of the night, Johnny did 12-5 and I did 1-6. During the morning I went Connell House for a swim and then returned to the ship for lunch. Cargo seemed to be very slow during the afternoon but even so we sailed at 1700.

Singapore – Port Swettenham.

Sunday 25th August – Monday 26th August.

I was for'ard for stand-by and once we were clear of the wharf I went round closing the watertight doors. Before chow John and I tightened the belly lines on the on the lifeboats. I did the 12-4 and we anchored off Swettenham at 0230. We stayed there until 0700 and then shifted to Deep Water point.

Port Swettenham.
Monday 26th August – Wednesday 28th August.

I went on the bridge to do the 12-4 anchor watch but unfortunately the Mate wanted two on so I did the 12-6 instead. There wasn't much to do except check the bearings and wait for calls on the VHF. At 1500 the Second Mate gave me a good job of sticking the naveams, W.F., W.U., W.M. and other notices into the scrapbook. This was finished about 1730. Cargo finished for the night at 2200 so no one was required for cargo or anchor watch.

I was called at 0500 to test the gear for stand-by for shifting our anchorage. The anchor was away at 0618 and we moored a little nearer to the wharf at 0715. The starboard anchor was let go and slacked off to 8 shackles and then the port anchor was dropped and we heaved up on the starboard cable until these were about four shackles in the water from each cable. We then started cargo at 0800 with one down #3 and one on deck. At 1400 we shifted again this time alongside for latex and the rest of our general cargo. We were all fast by 1530 and I had done the gangway stand-by. Taff and I were on again during the evening this time watching down #1 and #3. Five tanks of latex and one tank of coconut oil were to be loaded and by 2400 four tanks of latex and half the coconut oil had been loaded.

Cargo started at 0800 Wednesday morning but it almost immediately started raining and cargo did not start in earnest until after lunch. When Taff and I went on in the evening the #3 L.T.D. had nearly been filled and it was the last hatch to finish and we sailed at midnight. I was for'ard for stand-by and after I had done the watertight doors the Mate knocked me off.

Port Swettenham – Penang.
Thursday 29th August – Friday 30th August.
John and I were called at 0630 to clean the room. The Pilot was at 0915 and I did the ladder. We were supposed to go to a buoy, but when we'd broken the cable and lowered it to the waterline we were told the buoy wasn't available. We anchored at 10:30 instead.

Penang.
Thursday 29th August – Friday 30th August.
The three watchkeepers stayed on watch whilst John and I carried on with sixes until the return of Khong. No cargo was worked until after lunch because of the rain. John did the 12-6 and when I relieved him at 1830 he was in #3. Initially as they had reached the hatch coaming with the rubber stow. Khong returned before eight, so he and Johnny came on then. Taff and I were then called out to move a load of eggsticks from #4 which we finished about 2100. I was called for stand-by at 0200 and went on the gangway. I changed the Aldis battery before stand-by and just connected it before we commenced heaving up the anchor. The Pilot was away at 0306 and F.S.A. was 0315. The clocks were put back an hour then.

Penang – Aden.
Friday 30th August – Thursday 5th September.
We weren't called until breakfast, so now I'm well refreshed for the trip to Aden. After breakfast we collected a lot of dunnage, 3x3, from #4 to #1 and #2. We then helped Chippy Tom off down #1, #2 and #5. #5 was very awkward because the access had been blocked off and when we did get in there wasn't any dunnage so we lashed the stows.
We were called at 0530 Saturday and turned to scrubbing the teak wood rails on the Engineers deck. This took longer than I expected and about 0720 we started using Harpic which brought up the rails beautifully. We finished the rails after breakfast and then we moved four cases of lizard skin from

the port to the starboard fore cabin. They were damned heavy and worth about £3000. We then painted the winch on the aft starboard end of the Engineers deck. We finished the winch at about 1330 with 15 minutes for lunch. We had the rest of the afternoon off and I caught up with a lot of jobs that needed doing.

Saturday midnight we changed watches and I went on the 4-8. During the morning we picked up Ceylon on the radar. By 0830 we still couldn't see land. During the evening watch we passed *"Agapenor"* homeward bound and she looked cleaner than in Singapore, but still left a lot to be desired. She was abeam at 1600 and could not be seen at 1800. Monday morning we had picked up a little speed and we were doing 20.13 knots. At stars Minicoy had not been picked up at 0830. We were off Minicoy about 1100 and we were on bearings for noon. The sea is moderate with a long swell and the wind about Force 5 and it is sunny.

Tuesday morning the swell was a little bigger and the wind was force 6. We didn't see any ships in either 4-8. During the morning from 0900 to about 1015 the 4th Mate and I checked the hoses and fire extinguisher refills. Wednesday the weather is a little worse and our speed is down to about 19 1/2 knots. The wind Being about force 7 or 8 now. The weather is cooler and there are quite a few showers. Johnny, Taff and Khong are on day work and are working in the boats.

We picked up Socotra Wednesday evening and the weather improved. We passed the *"Flintshire"* outward bound at about 1940. She had four and a half thousand tons space, we have only two and a half thousand. We were out of the Lee of Socotra about 2300, but when I went on watch the weather had calmed down again and we were inside Gardafuey. During the evening watch we had a lot of ships but nothing much else. At 2000 we were 20 miles from the Pilot. For stand-by I was aft, it was an awful stand-by and I was cobby.

Aden.
Thursday 5th September – Friday 6th September.

We were all fast about 2200 and in the mail we had the latest edition of the halfdeck, which was strongly criticised, praised and quoted alternatively by all of us. With the perpetual repeat by someone of something you yourself read out five minutes before. I crashed at midnight and was called again at 0400 and thankfully cargo had finished at 0330. We unloaded from #1 and #6. Two were required for cargo until #6 finished. We tested gear at 0522. P.O.B. was 0645 and F.S.A. was 0651.

Aden – Suez.
Friday 6th September – Sunday 8th September.
As soon as we were clear we went on to 250 degrees and there were quite a few ships. We passed Perim Island about 1130. During the evening watch we had one alter course of five degrees. We were in Hell's Gate at 1600. Saturday morning we had quite a lot of ships and the wind was increasing to about force 5, but the temperature was still 90 degrees at 0800. During the evening watch nothing of note happened.

Sunday Johnny, Giles and I were on daywork whilst John, Khong and Taff went on watch. We were called at 0630 and Johnny and I cleaned out the room. After breakfast we turned to wire brushing the Aft starboard main deck when we had finished this the Bosun washed it down with salt and fresh water. In the afternoon we wiped the poop, docking bridge aft main deck over with thinners to remove the grease. Then, hooray, we painted them with grey primer. We anchored in Suez Bay at 2330.

Suez Canal Transit.
Monday 9th September.
Johnny and I were called at 0530 and we read our letters and then bailed out the last foot or so of the swimming pool so it would dry for some repairs to be done to it. Then after being caught by the Mate with my feet on the halfdeck table we took some fruit to the veg room. We commenced to weigh anchor at 0840 and Johnny and I went for'ard. After that we painted

distinguishing marks on the swimming pool stanchions and then painted the topping lift ratchet bars red. We anchored in the Bitter Lakes at 1245 and stayed there until about 1400. After lunch when we had finished the ratchet bars we started to scrape the port fore deck. It was very hot and not much enthusiasm was felt or displayed for the job. We passed the cut about 1630 but there weren't any Blueys in the southbound convoy. We arrived in Port Said at about 2100 and I was for'ard for stand-by. We weren't stopping but the ropes had to be put down. When the ropes were down I went round and checked the watertight doors and then turned in.

Port Said – London.
Monday 9th September – Tuesday 17th September.
Called at 0530 and we had to wash down the vents on the mast houses and paint them. It was quite an awkward job because the Mate didn't want any paint on deck and there was a high wind. When we finished that we washed down and painted #7 hatch and coaming. We finished this about 1615 only to be told by the Mate that it had taken too long.

Wednesday we turned to and at 0610 only to be told by the Mate that we had to work until 1700 for turning to late. He, of course, had forgotten the 'ovies' we had done the night before, round the coast and every weekend. We had to wash and paint #1 and #2 hatch coamings. When we had washed down we found out that there were only 5 gallons of grey paint left so we could only touch up. During the day we touched up #1, #2 and #3 hatch coamings. The weather is very pleasant indeed wind force 2 and temperature at 78 degrees. During the evening we were busy with our office work.

Thursday we were called at 0530 and turned to promptly at 0600 and then had to wait 10 minutes for the 2nd Bosun to come and give us our paint. We cut in the for'ard end of the Engineers deck before breakfast and then started touching up #5 and #6 hatch coamings. We did the port side first because the port deck was to be painted. At 1400 we finished #5 and nearly finished

#6 when we had to take the pool down. We finished it 1600 and then had boat and engine room fire drills. I Immediately hopped into the bath and was just starting to soak when John came down and said the Mate wanted to see Johnny, Taff and I. When we got to the bridge, we found that we had a signals test waiting for us. As time passed, it became apparent that we were a little rusty to say the least. At the end we had a short international code test which ended when Johnny was asked what 'X' meant and he replied 'Stop your intentions'. This had us in stitches and we then left the bridge with the promise of another test on Sunday. The weather is much colder now and the wind is stronger. Rain showers have made it seem even colder and haven't done the new paintwork much good.

Friday morning we turned to before breakfast, putting the swimming pool boards on the Engineers deck and then strung the canvas up to dry. After looking for buckets to wash down #4 prior to touching it up we found that they had already been washed. After breakfast we touched up #4 and finished it just before the sailors started to paint that part of the deck. After lunch we finished #6 and then started the dogs on the sea doors. We passed 'Gib' at twenty past five, we went in very close and could almost see the fellow signalling to us. The weather is much cooler now and this morning we changed into Blues.

Saturday we turned to before breakfast making the doors on the mushroom vents work. After breakfast we carried on painting the dogs on the watertight doors. We got our own trunks up at 1200 and during the afternoon we were busily doing office work and dhobi. Midnight Saturday we change watches and I went on the 8-12. When I went on watch Sunday morning, we were in the middle of the bay with the mist and fog patches. A Sight was taken at 1222, but the horizon was hardly visible. When I went on watch in the evening we had left Ushant and were halfway across the channel to Brixham. We sighted Start Point about 2130. We picked up the Pilot off Berry Point at 0039 after the clocks had been flogged at 2300.

When I went on watch in the morning we had just passed

the Royal Sovereign Light vessel. Dungeness was on the radar and we passed about 0945. Dover Harbour was abeam at 1015. We then came to the South Goodwin. We reduce speed at 1200 to pass through the North Edinburgh Channel and when Giles relieved me at 1230 we were almost abeam of Knock John fortress. We anchored off the Great Nore at 1300. Johnny, John and Taff were on daywork and spent the morning down #1 shifting mats. During the afternoon John cleaned the sextant and the rest of us began to round up our office work.

We commenced weighing anchor at 1945 and was away at 1948. When I went on the bridge at 2000, we had just passed #1 sea reach buoy. At 2030 we passed Southend and were called up by the signal station on the pier. At 2137 we changed Pilots at Gravesend after clearing quarantine and immigration. We commenced swing at 2250 and swing was completed at 2300. We ran lines to the lock at 2318 and we were all fast at 2337. We started to leave the lock at 2349 and we were all clear by 2400. We were all fast at 0030.

We put the mirrors away, telescopes and binoculars. Then I helped the 3rd Mate write up the slate. This was interrupted to bring the Mates wife's gear up from her car. After finishing the slate and a couple of other old jobs we turned in about 0215. The weather has been very pleasant all day, the temperature around 60 degrees Fahrenheit.

What We Learnt...

Change is as good as a rest and so we have a little coastal jaunt across to the continent and back before swinging west, through the Bay of Biscay, the Mediterranean and Suez before frolicking around the far east like any good English gentleman should for our next deep-sea adventure.

As many would know about the North Sea, fog was the prevailing weather and time was spent loading and unloading Pilots while doing the odd bit of cargo and a drydock pitstop to sandblast the hull. A little bit more responsibility was given when in drydock; mainly keeping people away from a turning prop. Not exactly something you could miss...

The swimming pool when up in the Med, once they had changed into 'Whites', it also turns out that they had air-conditioning in the halfdeck, which seems a bit of luxury to be given to a bunch of Midshipmen in my opinion. Lots overhauling of gear, woodwork was completed along with lifeboat reconditioning and repacking of stores which included –

in my mind at least – an insane amount of condensed milk, 109 tins in each boat... how many tiramisu, banoffee pie or fudge recipes do these lifeboats contain?

When not loading a diabetes inducing amount of condensed milk into lifeboats, they shifted cargo, watched cargo be loaded and discharged and moved dunnage about. I don't know what Chicken Essence is, and I don't want to, but maybe it is better than wet pig skins, who knows? And if anyone can tell me what eggsticks are, I would be grateful.

The main excitement of the trip to me was the stowaway at Singapore, but not any common stowaway but one from HMS Lion – a bona fide sailor gone AWOL. This part of the log was written in a very factual way to be very clear all procedures were followed correctly.

Little Wendy was mentioned in dispatches, not that she is that little now, but she has taken after her father and uncle by becoming an avid sailor in her spare time. And while P. J. Wood mentioned mucking about with ropes in the previous voyage, Wendy's claim to fame is that she can tie a bowline with her feet – a blast at all the parties I'm sure!

Proof that a radio was bought on the voyage – this is the actual instruction manual saved for historical purposes in P. J. Wood's old sea truck.

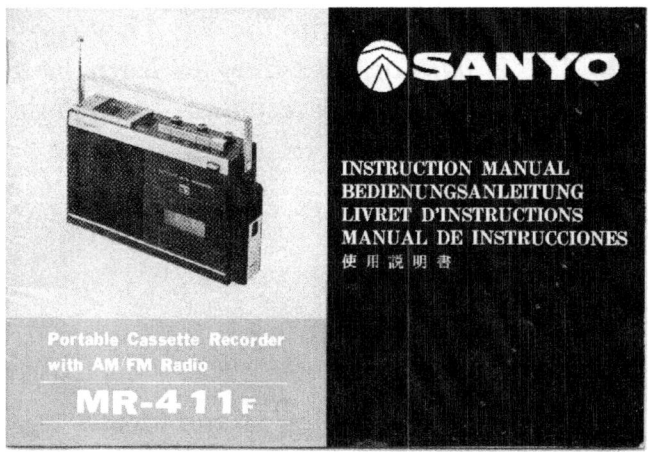

M.V. CLYTONEUS

October 1963
Voy. 40

Master: J. C. Liptrot
Mate: E. I. Grant
2nd Mate: D. P. Worsnop
3rd Mate: Peter. Bird
4th Mate: Howard W. Simmonds

Midshipmen
- P. J. Wood
- A. I. Hale
- J. L. Wilson
- J. R. K. Corrin

"In your dealings with the seaman and other ratings be civil and friendly but without unseemly familiarity. They can often teach you much and it is part of your duty to learn by sympathetic understanding of their lives how to obtain from those under you willing and efficient service."

- *Midshipman Appointment Letter from Alfred Holt & Co. circa 1960*

Voyage of M.V. Clytoneus - Map

Voyage Statistics

Monday 7th October 1963 - Birkenhead - Joined Ship

Friday 18th October 1963 - Port Said

Suez Canal Transit

Tuesday 22nd October 1963 - Jeddah

Saturday 26th October 1963 - Aden

Tuesday 5th November 1963 - Singapore

Friday 8th November 1963 - Penang

Monday 11th November 1963 - Port Swettenham (Port Klang)

Friday 15th November 1963 - Singapore

Wednesday 20th November 1963 - Djakarta (Jakarta)

Thursday 28th November 1963 - Palembang

Saturday 7th December 1963 - Djakarta (Jakarta)

Saturday 14th December 1963 - Belawan

Sunday 22nd December 1963 - Trincomalee

Thursday 2nd January 1964 - Djibouti

Monday 6th January 1964 - Suez

Suez Canal Transit

Wednesday 8th January 1964 - Port Said

Friday 17th January 1964 – London

Total number of Ports visited: 17
Total Voyage time: 102 days

Total Voyage Distance*: 18,772 Nautical miles

* All distances are estimated using Reed's New Maritime Distance Tables (1965) [Acquired from Fenton Steamship Co. Chartering and S&P department] and by going "old school" with Lloyds Atlas of World Shipping Ports (30th Edition). Ports, wharfs, jetties and buoys have all changed dramatically over the last 62 years so that calculating accurate distances is nearly impossible to determine, so we used our best judgement.

Films watched during voyage: 12
"The Defiant Ones" IMDB Score: 7.6 - released in 1958.
Middies Review: None
"Svengali" IMDB Score: 5.5 - released in 1954.
Middies Review: "It was a load of unadulterated bilge"
"A Private's Affair" IMDB Score: 5.4 - released in 1959.
Middies Review: "A corny Yankee comedy"
"Campbells Kingdom" IMDB Score: 6.4 - released in 1957.
Middies Review: None
"Taste of Fear" IMDB Score: 7.4 - released in 1961.
Middies Review: "I enjoyed"
"Follow That Horse" IMDB Score:5.6 - released in 1960.
Middies Review: None
"Time lock" IMDB Score: 6.0 - released in 1957.
Middies Review: None
"The Siege of Pinchgut" IMDB Score: 6.3 - released in 1959.
Middies Review: None
"Inn for Trouble" IMDB Score: 5.7 - released in 1960.
Middies Review: "We thought was damn good"
"The Chapman Report" IMDB Score: 5.5 - release in 1962.
Middies Review: "Wasn't so popular"
"Parrish" IMDB Score: 6.5 - released in 1961.
Middies Review: None
"The Sins of Rachel Cade" IMDB Score: 5.9 - released in 1961.
Middies Review: "Was very good and enjoyed by all"

Birkenhead.

Monday 7th October 1963 – Thursday 10th October 1963.

I joined the ship about 1645 to find that two other Middies had joined but were not on board. I did my unpacking and about 1800 went ashore I returned to the ship about 2300 to find one of the two first trippers aboard. The next day Ian, Bob and I reported to the office at 0900 and after our medical we were signed on in Birkenhead. O'Neills picked us up and after leaving our luggage on board, he took us back to the office. We had our interviews and collected our office work and logs during the afternoon and returned to the ship. We all went ashore during the evening.

Wednesday we had boat drill at 1000 and the inspection at 1430. We all went ashore afterwards. We were all called at 2300 for stand-by. I went on the bridge Ian went on the gangway Bob went aft and John went for'd. Stand-by went at midnight and we were all clear at 0024. At 0120 we were all fast in the locks and Ian came up and relieved me. We were called again at 0310 and I went to the bridge. We were all clear of the locks by 0350 when Ian came up and relieve me. F.S.A. was 0500. Chow was at 0730 and when I went on the bridge at 0800 Holyhead was in sight. The Pilot was away at 0857 and full speed away was 0900.

Birkenhead – Port Said.

Thursday 10th October – Friday 18th October.

When the Pilot was away, we started to keep the watches in the halfdeck. I was on the 8-12 and John and I took the trunks down and cleared out the halfdeck during the morning. During the afternoon we didn't have any jobs and we all spent a rather subdued afternoon thinking about home. During the evening I made a determined effort to raise our spirits and completely emptied my store of jokes, I succeeded on my own behalf and the others seemed a little happier. Friday we turned to after breakfast at 0815. Bob and I washed down the paintwork on the bridge. We then sand and canvassed the rails on the bridge and the Old Man's deck. After smoko we cleaned the brass and washed the windows on the bridge. There was a boat and fire drill at 1615.

Saturday it was too dark to turn to before breakfast and afterwards Bob and I washed down the bridge and boat decks whilst John cleared out the halfdeck. Then we cleared up some oil on the fiddely which took until after lunch. When we had finished we had the rest of the afternoon off, I did quite a bit of dhobi and this trip I hope to stay ahead of myself in that respect. No work on Sunday so quite a lot of office work was done. Passed Gib during the afternoon, the weather is noticeably better now, with temperatures in the 70s. We are still in Blues.

Monday we were called at 0630 and before breakfast we took the cover off #2 boat and took the oars, mast and sails out. After breakfast Bob cleaned out the halfdeck whilst Ian and I took all the gear out of the boat prior to tarring and painting it. By 1400 we were ready to start tarring so we collected the gear and started. We finished about 1700 and spent the hour before chow cleaning ourselves up. We were called at 0530 Tuesday morning and we sugied the bottom boards and tank cladding of #2 boat. After breakfast we sand and canvassed the oars and finished suugying. We then hung the sails up to air. After lunch Bob and I stretched out the pilot ladder and the manropes on #3 hatch and sugied and painted them whilst Ian and John painted the leading on #4 hatch. At 1600 they hadn't quite finished, so I helped Ian finish off. Afterwards we put the sails away. During the afternoon we passed Pantelleria and pass quite close to an aircraft carrier which seemed very big. The weather is still quite good.

Wednesday we turned to before breakfast sugying the paintwork inside #2 boat. We then sugied the mast of the boat. After breakfast Ian and I started painting it. The job was only half done when it started raining. During the afternoon the rain showers continued so we sugied all the grease marks off the paint on the boat deck. During inspection this morning the Old Man looked at the towels and to his horror and my surprise two of them were damn filthy so now we are dhobying our towels. Tonight there is 30 minutes on the clocks. Thursday before breakfast we washed down all of the buoyancy tanks for #2 Boat, overhauled the pump, ground the axes and made everything ready to oil the tanks and finish painting the boat. After breakfast I changed the Aldis battery whilst Ian did the vents. We had started painting the boat by smoko time after replacing the tanks and cleaning and then I went off on another job, finding keys for locks and vice versa. This job took me the rest of the day. Ian and Bob meanwhile finished off all they could do on the boat by 1400 and so they started cleaning the Bridge brass. After Smoko John went on the wheel for an hour. The weather is now warmer, but we are still in Blues. The clocks will be put forward 30 minutes tonight.

Friday morning we put all of the remaining gear back in the boat before breakfast. Ian and I barbarised the bridge before smoko being very careful to clear up all of the sand afterwards. At lunchtime the Mate told me that I would be doing a watch in place of one of the sailors who is sick. It turned out that he was on the 4-8, so I had the afternoon off whilst the others scrubbed out the wheelhouse and chart room, cleaned the bridge windows and scrubbed the Old Man's rail. We had boat and fire drill at 1615. I went on lookout at 1720 relieving Ian who had done 10 minutes whilst I had chow. I was relieved at 1815 and stand-by for anchoring was about 1835 we were knocked off until we moved in at 0040 on Saturday.

Port Said.
Canal Transit
Saturday 19th October – Sunday 20th October.

I was for'd for stand-by and we put out three ropes and a wire we were all fast by 0215. I was called again at 0600 and turned to bringing the boats on board and lowering the derricks. Stand-by for moving into the canal went about 0745 and after I had raised the gangway I went for'd. We were all clear by 0830 'En route' to the cut we passed through a minor sandstorm which left a thin film of sand over everywhere. We entered the cut about

1200 and stand-by went about 1225. I was aft and we put out three ropes. We were all finished by 1315 and we then watched the northbound convoy pass. Stand-by went again at 1745 and I went for'd for stand-by. I stayed up there until 1840 when I was relieved for chow. At 1900 I went on the wheel and was on when we passed through the bridge [Road bridge over the Suez Canal] and finished just as we had changed Pilots. The new Pilot was a bit of a head case and I wish I'd been on with him. We cleared the canal about 0100.

Port Said – Jeddah.
Sunday 20th October – Tuesday 22nd October.
I was on the first lookout at 0400. There were quite a few ships. At twenty past five, I went and woke up the stand-by man to relieve me. I went on the wheel at 0700 until 0800. We had one alter course to 135 degrees. At noon we reduced speed for a daylight arrival. During the afternoon we changed onto the 12-4. I was knocked off seaman's watches and, in the evening, as only two are required for each watch.

Monday we put the awnings up on the Bridge and the Boat deck. At 1030 we had emergency boat drill and we lowered boats #3 and #4. Ian and I went in #3 boat and we were away for about an hour after pulling a short distance and pulling up the mast and sails. Two ships came close to us for a close up of our regatta a 'Ben boat' and Texaco tanker. During the afternoon we squared up the boats and put the remaining awnings up. Tuesday we were called at 0700 by the Mate one to go on the bridge and the others into chow. I went on the Bridge and we were navigating through reefs. I did the movement book. P.O.B. was at 0735, and when Ian relieved me at 0750, we were just about to come to the awkward part. We did a running moor and we were brought up at 0824.

Jeddah.
Tuesday 22nd October – Thursday 24th October.
We were supposed to be in Jeddah a day, but as some of the

men had gone to fight in the Yemen, the rumours went around that it would be nearer four days. We were going to do most of the tallying and Tuesday we only unloaded the small amount of deck cargo from Port Said. Wednesday we were called at 0530 to start work at six. Unfortunately, no gangs turned up until about seven. We then split up with me tallying at #1, Bob at #2, Ian at #5, and John at #6. We were relieved for chow and smoko, but other than that we were all busy until 1530. The heavy lifts from #2 were only waiting for a lighter then there were some specials on deck at #1 also waiting for a lighter. Ian and I stayed on until 1830, by which time all the heavy lifts had gone from #2 and the starboard fore cabin was being unloaded. Cargo finished about 2030 and we were all off then until we sailed. We were called at 0530 and Bob and Ian went on the bridge. John and I went on the gangway. Ian was on the wheel. The Pilot was away by 0700.

Jeddah to Aden.
Thursday 24th October – Saturday 26th October.
Before breakfast I cleared the boat deck ready to wash down after which we washed down the decks and the bulkheads with salt water. We then helped the electrician clean the fan filters and soak them in oil. Bob and John cleaned the foc'sle bell before smoko. During the evening we put the table and chairs on deck on the port side lit with a cluster and then sat out there reading and writing. We have done this for the past two evenings and it is very pleasant. Called at 0530 Friday and replaced the fan filters. After which John scrubbed out the wheelhouse whilst Ian and I did some brass.

After breakfast I scrubbed the Old Man's rail and the bridge rail. I then began to scrub the ladder handrails. Finishing this was job and finish so Ian and I carried on with the brass. Bob and John came up straight after lunch and we finished about one o'clock. During the afternoon we did some dhobi and some letter writing. At about 1600 we passed through Hells Gates and we passed Perim at 2100 and I went on the wheel for the alter courses and until we were clear of most ships. We arrived in

Aden about 0400 Saturday and John and I were called for the pilot ladder and gangway. We're all fast by 0450.

Aden.
Saturday 26th October.
Only one was required so Ian volunteered to stay up. He called us for breakfast and afterwards only one Middy was needed. John did this and was knocked off at 0900. None of us were required then until stand-by, so most of our energies went into bargaining with the bum boats. Stand-by went at 1150 and there was a bit of a rush to get clear before the P&O passenger ship "*Himalaya*[35]". We did get clear before her and then passed the four Japanese destroyers which recently visited Britain. I was on the wheel and stayed on until we steadied up on 096 degrees at about 1245. We had the rest of the day off and I did a lot of dhobi and the library. We passed "HMS Albion[36]" about 1500 inward bound to Aden.

Aden – Singapore.
Saturday 26th October – Tuesday 5th November.
During the evening we nearly all read. We changed watches at midnight and I am to go on the 12-4. Nothing eventful happened during the morning watch Sunday, but during the afternoon we passed Guardafui and sighted the Brothers [El Ikhwa Islands]. Even though we were on bearings we took two latitudes and a longitude star in the evening. Monday morning also passed uneventfully and after taking a noon sight the rains came so I stayed on the bridge as lookout. Ian, Bob and John painted the deckhead in the halfdeck. Tuesday morning we passed the "*Pyrrhus*[37]" and after smoko I had a go at working out the previous evening stars. I took a morning sight and as usual and went up for noon. During the afternoon Bob and I painted the cladding and mast of #4 boat whilst Ian and John tarred and painted the boat. I took stars again this evening and I'm just about getting the hang of them. No different really from a sun sight.

Wednesday morning I couldn't work out my stars and nothing untoward happened. During the afternoon Bob John and I washed out the wheelhouse and oiled the buoyancy tanks. Thursday morning we were in sight of Minicoy at midnight and had already altered course to 107 degrees. We were abeam at 0110. I worked out my stars after smoko and they came out rather well. The afternoon was spent scrubbing and painting the ladder handrails on the starboard side amidships and the ladder leading up to the poop. Last night we had a small fire in the paint locker which turned out to be a drum of waste. It was thrown over the side immediately and no damage was done.

Friday morning we expected to sight Pt Galle in our watch but it wasn't sighted until the 4-8. We were on bearings for noon. During the afternoon we chipped, scraped and red leaded some rails on the poop and finished painting the handrails on the ladders. Saturday morning we had a lot of rain on the 12-4, but otherwise the watch was uneventful. During the afternoon I had to keep an eye on a deck boy learning to steer and John who didn't really need it. During the evening I did some office work and carried on with the cargo plan the Mate gave us to complete. Sunday we didn't have any jobs so I did some office work, dhobi, covered some books and finished the cargo plan. The weather has been showery all day and this afternoon when we altered to 105 degrees entering the Malacca Straits it was raining hard.

Monday was not my day. I was up late and then started badly on the job of sugying the boat deck. The job didn't go quickly and it took us, or me, all day just to do the boat deck bulkheads and the deck head on the Old Man's deck. Crashing early tonight for a good start tomorrow. Today it has been foggy nearly all day. We were called at 0530 and I went on the wheel for arriving in Singapore. We picked up the Pilot about 0645 and we were alongside by 0800. Taking a long time to get alongside and a very trying quarter of an hour going from hard a' starboard to hard a' port.

Singapore.

Tuesday 5th November – Thursday 7th November.

The Mate wanted two on so John and I stayed on until twelve o'clock. The Mate also wanted one of the seniors on the night. I did the first night and during the afternoon Ian and I went ashore and had a haircut and did some shopping. Nothing happened during the night which was worth noting. Wednesday I was on the afternoon and we worked among other things the strong room which the 4th Mate and I had to sort carefully. During the evening I went ashore and did some more shopping. I was on Thursday morning and kept one eye on #1, #2 and #3 as there are two Mates and two Middies on there isn't much to do. I had the afternoon off and went ashore shopping.

Friday morning I was on that night. At 0400 I went for'd and sensed something was wrong. The moorings were alright, then I realised the deck was radiating heat. I couldn't see any flames or smoke though keyhole of the fore cabin door, so I assumed it was something to do with the windlass I called the Lecky and the 3rd Mate, got the fore cabin key and we went for'd. On opening the door, there was a very heavy smell of scorched paint, plus a little smoke which attacked the eyes. We walked for'd and just beside the contacts for #2 winch the heat was at its fiercest. The Lecky found that one of the contacts hadn't broken when the winch was switched off. The "panic" was over, but the contact had to be repaired. For one and a half hours the Lecky and I sweated cobs whilst he fixed the contact and I held the torch. When it was all over we nearly froze going back to the accommodation and he didn't even buy us a beer. I was on again in the afternoon until 1600 when we went on sea watches. We sailed at 1730 Friday and I was on the gangway until the Pilot was away at 1810.

Singapore – Penang.
7th November – 8th November

I then had chow and relieved Ian on the wheel. I stayed on the wheel until 2030 when we had just altered course off Raffles Light. We arrived in Penang during the evening and at 1830 I went on the wheel. We were alongside by 2000.

Penang.
Friday 8th November 1963 – Monday 11th November.

John and Ian stayed on until midnight, one watching #1 and the other on deck. There is a great deal of over stowed cargo and with the mail as well three Mates were required as well. At midnight when Bob and I went on I was given charge of the aft hatches. Not much happened and I was able to cope easily with some assistance from the 2nd Mate now and again. I crashed very soon after six in the morning. When I came out at 1200, cargo had stopped until 1300. The "*Cathay*[38]" which was ahead of us, sailed at 1230 and we moved one of our headlines for her. During the afternoon, Bob and I took turns watching down #1. We were to sail that night, so to even things out I went on watch again at 2000, relieving Ian who was to go on the wheel. Long lengths of steel had to be unloaded from #5 starboard deck and after unloading two rather awkwardly cargo was finished in the hatch and then the hatch was closed and the beams were unloaded. I tested the gear with 3rd Mate at 2300 and we sailed at 0100. I was in charge of the gangway, which was easy because we had a short gangway and the Pilot left about 0230 after taking us out via the South Channel. I turned in about 0300.

Penang – Port Swettenham.
Monday 11th November.

We were called at 0730 and turned to after breakfast cleaning out the halfdeck. When this was finished we had the rest of the morning off. At 1130 I went on the wheel and the Pilot was on board at 1200. We anchored astern of the "*Menestheus*[39]" and there were another 14 ships ahead of us. We were anchored by 1400.

Port Swettenham.
Monday 11th November – Friday 15th November.

We were given the rest of the day off which we spent relaxing and writing letters. Tuesday we were called at 0530 by John, who had been on the 12-6 gangway watch and we turned to washing the paintwork inside the wheelhouse. We had started painting the deck head by 1100 and we had really got going by lunchtime. I had the afternoon off as I was on the 6-12 gangway watch. Ian and Bob finished off the wheelhouse by 1500, whilst John had been repairing the Malayan courtesy flag. The monsoon struck with full fury at 1800 hours, just as I was doing the lights and flags. The film "The Defiant Ones" with Tony Curtis was shown during the evening. John was again on the 12-6.

Wednesday we finished the bulkheads and painted some of the instruments, we were given the afternoon off to go ashore swimming, which we accepted with reservation, waiting for the catch. We had another film during the evening this time it was "Svengali" and it was a load of unadulterated bilge. I crashed at the end of the first reel and was thankful to do so. I was on the 6-12 and John on the 12-6. Thursday was Prince Charles' birthday but it also happens to be mine. So Ian and I were going ashore. During the day we finished the wheelhouse and at 1615 when we knocked off, we were satisfied with our work. At 1700 hours we asked the 6th and 7th engineers for a bit of a celebration. They bought a record player and some drinks. Beer for themselves, the main reason being that they are restricted to two a day. At about 1730 the Mate walked in and said shore leave had been cancelled as we were probably sailing to Singapore at 0100 the next day. Three whistles then went and the Mate wanted to see me whereupon he mournfully told me that engineers weren't allowed in the halfdeck. Neither is anybody else, but we aren't allowed anywhere, so we have to sit in this abhorrent little festering set of uninsulated bulkheads just because people misinterpret some bloody archaic set papers we signed before we knew better. The union will, of course, have a complaint or two next January or February. We turned in early and were called at 2400 for stand-by. Bob and I going onto the gangway, we were all clear by 0230 and Bob and I finished by 0300.

Port Swettenham – Singapore.

Friday 15th November.

We were called at 0800 and turn to after chow cleaning the wheelhouse. During the afternoon, Bob and Ian finished the brass and I went on the wheel at 1400. We anchored in the roads at 1630 in quite a crowded position. At 1730 we weighed anchor and shifted to another anchorage stern first We were brought up at 1830.

Singapore.
Friday 15th November – Wednesday 20th November.

During the evening we read and wrote letters. Next day Ian replaced the handrails on the poop ladder and we then painted the rails around the ladder well and at smoko had the charming company of Riley the math girl. We then sand and canvassed the Old Man's rail. At 1700 stand-by was for moving alongside, Ian and Bob were on the Bridge. We passed the "Glenogle[40]" as she was about to anchor in the roads we were all fast by 1830. John and I were on during the evening and we unloaded Guinness from #1, steel from #2, cars from #3, general from all the rest. Ian was on the night.

Bob and I were on the next morning and at 1000 we were singled up. Bob knocked off and I was on again Monday 12-6 so in the meantime I did some shopping and swimming. Monday afternoon Ian and I did some shopping but I managed to spend very little money. During the evening, Ian and I went to Connell House to see the film "Privates Affair" a corny Yankee comedy. We picked up some magazines at the mission and returned to the ship about 2300 hours.

Tuesday morning I had to go down #6 to try and make the hatch cleaners clean it properly. I was on the gangway for leaving with John. The Pilot left by the gangway, so by 2400 when we had unrigged and lashed it, we were able to turn in.

Singapore – Djakarta.
Wednesday 20th November – Thursday 21st November.

We turned to in the morning, stretching the log line.

Unfortunately it was not as strong as we anticipated, so it is now stretched beyond repair. During the afternoon we coiled two 80 fathom and one 90 fathom wire into #5 locker and then did a few odd jobs under the Bosun. Next morning we were called at 0530 and after putting all the hoses in a 'safe' places we went to turn in the gangway. I cut my thumb trying to remove a broken bulb from the gangway light. After breakfast we arrived off Djakarta and I was on the wheel for stand-by. Afterwards we turned to turned to with the Bosun topping derricks and unrigging the fore 'stay. At smoko when I took the glove off my hand with the cut thumb blood was dripping from the dressing so the Mate had knocked me off. That evening I did the 6-12 anti-pirate patrol and repelled these would be boarders. "Campbells Kingdom" was shown during the evening.

Djakarta.
Friday 22nd November – Wednesday 27th November.

The next morning we were supposed to move in at 0600 and so typically the Pilot arrived at 0830. I went on the wheel again for stand-by and it took us two and a half hours to get alongside. The Mate wanted two on again during the day. Bob and I went on at 1830. The Mate came along at about 2000 and said two Middies would be going on a trip to the mountains Saturday and two on Sunday. I knocked Bob off at 2030 after we had washed down some potassium permanganate which had spilled out of some drums in the port fore cabin.

Midnight Friday, John came on and we were working cargo. We worked from 0000 till 1800 between us, I did 0600 to 1800. The day was very hot and I was very shocked to hear President Kennedy of the U.S.A. had been assassinated. The Yankee or I should say "Ret" Ship "*Doctor Lykes*[41]" was in the berth opposite and we put our ensign at half-mast in respect. During the day we unloaded from all hatches and already I'm cheesed off with Java. Bob and Ian arrived back about 1900 after a very good day in the mountains. They were loaded down with 'percussion instruments' of all sorts, some of which I must buy tomorrow.

Sunday John and I went to the mountains with the Vicar, the 4th and the Senior Leckie. It took about two hours to get there and in the process we were impressed by the scenic quality of the country. When we arrived we went straight to the pool, which was full but pleasantly so. The 'talent' was pretty good and I'm glad my body is a bit brown because I felt less conspicuous. We stayed until about 1500 when we came back to the ship this time though Djakarta itself. We saw the burnt-out British Embassy, which isn't a heap of ruins as the British newspapers make out. We also saw the 'GANEFD' Stadium which was very modern (GANEFD means games of the new forward-looking people or something) John was on when we returned.

I was on midnight and no cargo was being worked. Nothing eventful happened. I was on again after lunch as the Mate now wants 3 on during the day and one on during the evening and night. It has to work so that the evening man has the afternoon off and the morning fellow has the evening off not very satisfactory, but it will have to do. Most of the time is spent testing wells and scuppers and we have started mucking about with the deep tanks. Tuesday I was on all day and as #3 for'd port and starboard tanks had been okayed by the surveyors at noon we filled them for ballast. I was on till 2000 when the tanks were filled and then did a quick change to watch the film "Taste of Fear", which I enjoyed. Wednesday morning Ian and I had to sweep the dust up in #6 for the surveyor to look at the D.B. tanks. We found that the hatch needed a clean, let alone a sweep. Before this was finished the Mate came down and I was told to go and harden up #3 port and starboard deep tanks. This took about an hour and then I was on deck. The decks everywhere are heaped with dust, mats, smashed dunnage and beer cans. Very Inconvenient as well as unhealthy. Stand-by went at 1730 and I was on the gangway. As soon as the pilot ladder was rigged, I had my chow in the duty mess. The Pilot was away at 1845.

Djakarta to Palembang.
Thursday 28th November 1963.

I was on the 12-4 and as we have 100 bajos on board I made frequent fire patrols. They were though all fast asleep under #5 and #6 hatch tents. During the morning Ian, John and Bob did various jobs including making the motor lifeboat ready for lowering. At 1130 we all went with 3rd Mate in the lifeboat to pick up some mail from the "*Agapenor*" and give them some small packages for Surabaya. We then proceeded to the entrance of the Musi River. We anchored at 1330 and almost immediately the Pilot boarded and said we could go in immediately. Bob and I were on the bridge for a while and then Bob knocked off. Only one of the seniors being required on the bridge. Ian relieved me at 1600, and when I relieved him at 1830 we had just anchored off Gungei Garong. We thought we would be here all night, but we heaved up again at 2000 and moved to an anchorage off Palembang. We were brought up at 2115 and then I turned in for the 12-4. We had a bit of strife today, the outcome being that we are now not allowed to use a lounge when the bar is closed. For this small mercy we are grateful, but if we were allowed to sign for two ales a day all this strife would be ended. Take note and ACT!

Pelambang.
Thursday 28th November – Thursday 5th December.
Good deck patrol has to be kept up to keep pirates away. During the morning we didn't have any attacks or even near misses to our knowledge. We shifted ship again during the morning and started cargo. I was on the 12-6 watching and supervising down #1. We were loading rubber into the orlop deck. The cargo to be watched was in the tween deck, and lo and behold it was being pinched from basically behind my back. I tried to stop them but was held by a lot of blokes around the ladder and on the squares. By the time I reached the main deck the empty sack, which had contained small tyres, have been thrown back into the tween deck. I immediately reported the matter to the 2nd Mate who was standing at #2 and he told me to go down and sit on the rest of the sacks. This was not the last I heard of the matter. We

shifted alongside at 1700 and were all fast by 1830. When Bob relieved me cargo hadn't started.

Saturday I was on the 6-12 in the morning and cargo started 0800. I was for'd and Ian aft. We loaded coffee into #2 L.H. and continued with the rubber in #1 O.D. Coffee and rubber were also loaded in #5 and #6. During the evening we saw the film "Follow That Horse!".

Sunday I did the 12 -6 and at 0300 the 3rd Mate and I took soundings. Nothing else of note happened. When I woke up at midday I had received a cable to say I had another niece. Good news. During the evening 6-12 no cargo was worked and the aft peak was being emptied and I had to sound that regularly. It was empty eventually at 0100 Monday.

During the afternoon 12-6 we started loading option coffee in #2 L.H. which will be shifted again in Djakarta. Plenty of separation was needed on top of the London coffee. During the evening we saw the film "Time Lock".

I was on the morning Tuesday and we shifted ship at 0800. We shifted again at 1300 and for this I was on the Bridge. Wednesday morning we took soundings again this time at 0500. Rain started about 1100 and continued right through stand-by for shifting from the wharf at 1430. I was on the wheel and after a lot of mucking about we were brought up with three shackles in the water by 1645. I was on cargo during the evening and supervised loading in #2 T.D. whilst also watching the tea. At midnight Ian was required on the bridge so John relieved me in #2. Ian and I were on the wheel all the way down the Musi River and stand-by for weighing anchor was at 1145. We were supposed to have sailed at 1000. I was on the wheel for the first two hours and it was a very interesting wheel as well. steering by trees and atop huts. At 1545 when I went to relieve Ian, we were just anchoring and I went aft. We were brought up with three shackles in the water at 1600. Immediately several boats were alongside selling monkeys, parrots, pineapples and coconuts. During the evening and morning we stayed on sea watches to keep an anti-pirate patrol. The whole ship was infested with "beasties" which made a silent approach impossible.

We heaved up at 0830 and followed a tanker out of the river. We were clear of the river by 1000 and the Pilot was away by at 1045.

Palembang – Djakarta.
Friday 6th December – Saturday 7th December.

I went to the wheel again at 1030 and was on until we were steadied up on 135 degrees at 1100, we had the rest of the morning off. During the afternoon we cleaned #5 starboard lockers and nailed dunnage to the bulkheads. I should say the wooden slats on the bulkheads. Then we laid down 'duo papan' (note the Malay which is needed here, none of this 'I took my bicycle to Kuala Lumpur for repairs') Double dunnage and then knocked off at 1645. During the evening I did a pile of dhobi and soon I may catch up with myself. Saturday morning was called to go on the Bridge for arriving and we let go at 0500.

Djakarta.
Saturday 7th December – Wednesday 11th December.

The Pilot came on board it 0735 after playing "Eenie Meenie Miney Moe" with the ships at anchor. I had a quick chow and went on the wheel. We proceeded in at 0815 and we only had one tug which seemed to make the Pilot very slow. We swung and went down the dock stern first and we were all fast by 0945. There are three Middies on watches and myself on daywork. We unloaded rubber from #1, #2, #5 and #6 for trans-shipment to the states during the afternoon I was mainly involved with testing #3 aft deep tanks ballast line and then screwing the lid down.

I turned to at eight o'clock and went down #2 hatch watching the tea and personal effects in the tween deck. During the afternoon I put a head on #7 D.B. tank for the surveyor. I then was on deck until 1700. Bob was a little 'off colour' this evening so he had been knocked off and the rest of us are on sea watches. I'm on the 4-8.

Monday morning I relieved Ian in #2 again and at 0500 the gang knocked off. I then kept a deck patrol until they opened up again at about 0745. I started to put a head on #6 port D.B. During the evening watch when the gangs knocked off I stood at the top of the gangway searching them all for coffee. By the time I had finished we had collected about two cwts broached coffee. I wasn't very popular with the lads after that.

Tuesday morning no cargo was worked until 0800 so between 4-8 I scrubbed the gangway, did a few chores and called the others. After breakfast I went down the engine room to organise the pumping out of #6 port D.B. tank. On looking in the tank I found only about 10 buckets full of water in the whole tank. After this I took some talcum powder to #1 for the crepe rubber in the Orlop Deck. I was just about to have a shower when I had finished this when the Mate came in and I had to go and relieve the S.O.S. on gangway for an hour. During the evening watch we Loaded into #2 and #6 but were still discharging New York rubber from #5. I had another purge at the gangway, but this time managed only about three quarters of a hundredweight.

Wednesday morning cargo was being worked again and I relieved Ian in #5 where tea was being loaded into the tween deck. As soon as cargo was finished, it began to get light so I scrubbed the gangway. During the day we loaded rubber into #1, #2, #5 and #6. When I went on watch at 1600, we had just started loading into #2 tween deck. When two other marks had been loaded, by 2000, they knocked off and we tested gear at 2015. I was on the gangway for stand-by and the Pilot was away by 2210.

Thursday we weren't called until breakfast and afterwards we took all the dunnage out of #5 port lockers, swept it out and hosed it down. We then rigged a windsail and opened the scuttles to give it a good ventilation, we also washed down the bridge and boat deck. In the afternoon we sorted out some suitable dunnage for the lockers and then set to on the bridge cleaning brass and glass. The weather has been much cooler today and we've had a few rain showers.

Djakarta – Belawan.
Wednesday 11th December – Saturday 14th December.

We were called at 05:30 Friday and turn to painting the for'ard contactor house. We painted some white and put on a second coat of red lead on the first. We had finished this by lunchtime so we then helped the Bosun with a few odd jobs whilst the sailors were putting up a bulkhead in #5 L.H. to take bulk palm kernels. We had a boat drill at 1615.

Saturday we were called for breakfast and we then turned to putting a coat of white over the red lead. We were now anchored off Belawan and great interest was being taken in #3 for'ard D.T.'s which have been waxed for latex. we were often disturbed to do small jobs and we didn't finish until 1300.

Belawan.
Saturday 14th December – Thursday 19th December.

We had the rest of the afternoon off, so I took the opportunity to clean out my drawers and wardrobe and to air my gear. It was very hot day with a little wind. Stand-by went for moving alongside at 1600 and I was on the gangway with John. We were going port side to so we had to turn out and rig that gangway, we were all organised in about half an hour. We were all fast alongside by 1830. We didn't start Cargo right away and we had a film show "The Siege of Pinchgut". One Middy was wanted on all the time from 2300, so we split it between us. We started cargo at 0800 and I was on the 8-12. We discharged from #1 and #5 and then shifted cargo in #1 and #2.

We didn't work any cargo Sunday evening and we had a double feature film show, the first being "Inn for Trouble" which we thought was damn good and the second was "The Chapman Report" which wasn't so popular. Monday cargo started at 0800 again and we loaded tea into #2 T.D. which was where I spent the 0800-1130. During the evening cargo was worked until 2130 and I was supervising #2 again. Another film was shown during the evening this was "Parrish".

Tuesday, we shifted ship in the morning and started loading our five tanks at noon. We went on to sixes then as two of us were required, one on deck and one with the Mate. When Ian and I went on at 1800 the second tank of palm oil was just about finished. At 2130 it was all screwed down and sealed and the Mate said we could single up again. I knocked Ian off and by midnight the first tank of latex had finished and had been sealed up.

Wednesday we shifted ship again in the morning and we were supposed to start #3 after D.T. at 0900, then 1100, eventually it started at 1300. That evening a dance was held and I had the best job since I've been at sea, changing the records. No one danced and it was all over by 2215 and I then relieved Ian who was helping Chippy to screw up the D.T. No other cargo was worked all night.

Thursday morning we worked bottle into #5 lockers and I spent the morning moving my gear into the owner's cabin to make room for an Indonesian Middy who is going to join sometime before we sail. He arrived before lunch and unpacked his gear. I did the 12-4 and will now be on it all the way home. We were supposed to sail at 1600, but the Pilot didn't arrive until 1640 and then we had to wait for two ships to come in. We were eventually clear of the wharf by 1715. I was on the wheel until we had steadied up on 323 degrees at 0645. The Pilot was away at 06. 15.

Belawan – Trincomalee.
Thursday 19th December – Sunday 22nd December.
Tonight was my first night at sea in a single berth cabin and it was the height of luxury, lights out was lights out and there was quietness all around. Somewhere I can have some privacy, put my books and photos on the lashings of shelf room. You can put the community part of life in the halfdeck where the monkey put his nuts. When I went on watch midnight we were on bearings with Diamond Point and we altered to 284 degrees abeam of the light at 0125. Nothing much happened for the rest

of the watch. During the morning of Friday we were on bearings with Pulau We and noon was our last bearing we altered to 280 degrees at noon. The weather is much cooler now and we had a few showers during the afternoon. The vessel is rolling a little and Rita, the Indonesian, is very seasick.

Saturday morning nothing went well with my error, but I eventually managed to work it out. Noon was at 1204 and I had everything worked out quickly and accurately. The 2nd Mate and I checked the accuracy of all the navigational gear during the afternoon.

Sunday morning my error came out almost within 3 minutes and after that there was nothing much to do. At 0900 we took a sight and found that we were 10 astern and about 6 North as we suspected. Bearings weren't picked until 1257. I went on the wheel at 1330 and we made slow progress into the pilot station. Commander Hooper was aboard at 1457 and we were all fast at 1515.

Trincomalee.
Sunday 22nd December – Friday 27th December.
One was required for the night so Ian will be doing it. There is to be a film show tonight, so here comes a little rest? The film, "The Sins of Rachel Cade", was very good and enjoyed by all. Monday Cargo started unexpectedly at 0800 and as one was required Ian stayed on board whilst the rest of us went for a picnic and a swim in the lifeboat. It was very hot in the sun, but with the cool breeze it was very pleasant. We found a good place for a picnic and went exploring. The boat came back to the ship at lunchtime to pick up the 7th Engineer, so I came back and relieved Ian. During the afternoon we spent three hours waiting for the lighters and then managed to load about six slings into #3 tween deck before 1600. During the afternoon Christmas Eve, the pace was much the same, with one gang and one hatch working. During the evening, not much happened, but it was improved by the luxury of a single berth and some privacy to write letters.

Christmas Day.

The day started at 0800 when I was called for chow. After which some of us went ashore in the motor lifeboat to go to church. We left the ship at 0930 and were ashore by 1000 after being pretty well soaked in the journey. We looked around for a church and eventually found one, but there wasn't a service scheduled. The Vicar, though, was very obliging and agreed to conduct and said communion. When this was over, we chatted for a little and then returned to the launching stage. The 3rd and 4th Mates and the 4th Engineer weren't there, so we hung around for about half an hour. We eventually returned to the ship at noon and the sight of the "*Anchises*[42]" and "*Clytoneus*[43]" together was pretty good. We were flying DFD, GUB, PVP, Christmas Greetings to all vessels and it looked 'pretty smart'. I had a couple of hours crash during the afternoon to gain some strength for the evening's activities. I got up at 1600 to have a bath and clean my shoes etc, but the boat was just returning so I gave them a hand to raise it. After this I had my bath and then was roped in to serve chow in the Seaman's mess. This was quite a laugh and took about 40 minutes. We then changed and went into the lounge for 'hors d'oeuvres'. Chow was at seven o'clock and we had about five toasts, including one from John, the Merchant Navy, and lasted until 2015. It was a damn good chow and I nearly worked through the menu. Afterwards we returned to the lounge until 1130. We then bade farewell and not long after we were in the sevenths room. I turned in about 3 o'clock after a very enjoyable evening.

Cargo started in earnest Boxing Day and two are required. one in each hatch. When I relieved Ian London tea was being loaded in number #3 T.D. and when this was finished, Rotterdam was started in the centre castle, they had finished their quota by 1130 so the day knocked off then. I stayed on until 1830.

Friday morning when I relieved at midnight tea was going at quite fast pace into #3. By 0500 the tween deck was full and the starboard centre castle alleyway had just been started. At 0600 when I handed over to Ian, there was only one more lighter for #3, and #4 had finished.

Trincomalee – Djibouti.
Friday 27th December 1963 – Thursday 2nd January 1964.

I turned in at 0630 and was woken at 1030 for inspection. We were underway and F.S.A. had been at 0906 when I went on watch at noon we were on bearings and stayed on them all watch. I put her down about every 30 minutes and the 2nd Mate checked the bearings. That evening I started my office work in real earnest. At midnight we were all still on bearings and we were until about 0330. Noon on Saturday and we were rolling easily, the Indonesian was seasick again and sits down at every opportunity. We sighted a couple of ships during the afternoon and the juniors did an hour each on the wheel. Sunday morning we expected to see Minicoy at 0204 but it didn't come up until 0215. On the rising bearing, we were four miles north of the line. At 0315 we altered course to 280 degrees and at 0332 we were abeam.

During Sunday afternoon, we again sighted only a couple of ships, and the juniors did an hour each on the wheel. Monday morning it was decidedly cooler and the weather is moderating. I again kept a lookout while the 2nd Mate did his charts. Monday afternoon I coloured two complete cargo plans between one and four and during the evening I carried on with my office work. Tuesday morning there was still a long northeasterly swell and we were rolling, but slowly. During the afternoon I carried on with the cargo plans and did another three complete and two port plans. We had finished the lot by 1700.

New Year's morning wasn't very different from any other, except in wishing all and sundry a Happy New Year. The "*Oronsay*[44]" called us up and we exchanged greetings. At 0300 we turned the radar on, but we didn't pick up any land by 0400. By 0800 we had picked up the Brothers and we had Guardafui for noon. At 1505 we altered on to 268 degrees and I spent all afternoon correcting the Light List, Volume J. Thursday morning, the weather was much improved, though it was overcast. I had to take two errors as my first was a little out and the clouds broke up so I could do them.

Thursday morning we had very little to do and it was much cooler. 72 degrees was the temperature. for the watch. At 0900 I took a sight which put her one mile ahead. I carried on with the Light List until 1500. We sighted RAS BIR Lighthouse at 1505. At 1600 we were nearly abeam. At 1715 I went on the wheel for entering Djibouti. We anchored about 1805 and we waited to see what would happen.

Djibouti.
Thursday 2nd January 1964 – Friday 3rd January 1964.
The Pilot boat came alongside at 1905 but the chap who boarded wasn't the Pilot, he was the agent without the mail. There were more than enough volunteers to man the motor lifeboat to go ashore to collect the mail, so by 2000 we were on our way. We were back by 2100 and strange to relate I had two letters. I was not required on the 12-4 and we proceeded in at 0600. For stand-by I was on the gangway. We were finished on the gangway by 0715 and then two were required on deck. During the morning I wrote some letters. At noon when I relieved Ian, there were about 15 cattle still to load and some bags of chili's for London in #1. Cargo and oil was finished at 1315 and stand-by went about 1325. I was on the wheel until 1445 and we were then steering 056 degrees.

Djibouti – Suez.
Friday 3rd January – Monday 6th January.
F.S.A. was at 1400 and altered course off RAS BIR Lighthouse at 1330. I took a vertical sextant angle for distance off and a bearing when we were abeam. Somebody had to be ready for the wheel from 1600 until 1830. I stood by until 1700, when Ian took over. We were not required on the wheel as it turned out. The next morning during my watch we went through Hells Gates and I was at the wheel as soon as I went up. We had about

four alter courses in about an hour. When we were steadied on 291 degrees I came off the wheel. Saturday afternoon I carried on with correcting all of the Light Lists. We saw quite a few ships and the watch passed quickly. Sunday morning we could see Daedalus Reef when we came on watch. It was abeam at 0127, but we had altered at 0115. It is much cooler now and we wore sweaters on watch. During the afternoon the weather freshened and quite a lot of spray came over the cows. By 1000 the wind was about force 5 and at 1015 we reduced. During the afternoon I carried on with the Light Lists. At 1330 we increase speed to 110 revs and at 1600 to 115.

The next morning, it was much colder, the temperature dropping to 61 degrees. We changed into Blues at breakfast but not too soon, I already had my dose of pre-docking flu. During the morning we tested the steering gear and we reduced to do it. The total time taken up was 18 minutes. During the afternoon I polished off my third Light List and took a sight and error. We arrived in Suez at about 2145 and I was called for the pilot gear at 2245. We started to discharge the cows immediately and completed discharge by 0330. Situmeang was to go at 0400, but he just kept a deck patrol.

Suez Canal Transit.
7th January – 8th January.
Port Said.
As Ian and I wanted to do some steering in the canal, we went on watches with the seaman. Ian 8-12 and I 12-4. When we were on stand-by we had to repair the bridge dodgers. I was on the second wheel so from 1200-1300 I carried on with the dodgers. At 1250 stand-by went and we commenced heaving immediately the anchor was away by 1300. I was relieved at 1400 and went on the wheel again at 1500. At 1800 we were in the Bitter Lakes. When I went on at midnight, I relieved Ian for'ard. Stand-by went for stopping at Port Said about 0050 and I stayed for'ard to answer the phone. Two were required so John and I did the 12-6. They were very fast but so much sorting had

to be done then it averaged out a very slow discharge. When we finished at 0600 well over half the cargo had gone and hopes were high for a speedy departure. When I was called again at 1100 #4's rubber had been very slow because it was sticking despite the lashings of talc that was used. Eventually it finished at 1430. And stand-by went about 1450. I was on the wheel for stand-by and we were all clear by 1645. As soon as we were steadied on 321 degrees the 'iron mike' was switched on.

Port Said – London.
Wednesday 8th January – Friday 17th January.
The weather is noticeably cooler now and woollens are coming out at great rate of knots. Thursday morning I did some more Light List corrections and the 2nd Mate forgot to put the clock back until 0230 so after my smoko it was still 0200. Thursday morning we took a sight and it took me quite a while to work it out, it must be this cold in my head. During the afternoon I kept a lookout whilst the 2nd Mate did his NEMREDRI [Bridge paperwork]. I took an error, but it was all wrong. Friday morning we went through the Malta Straight and the Old Man was on the bridge for most of the watch. Next afternoon the weather seemed a little warmer but I think we were just getting acclimatised. I kept a lookout and did another Light List. Saturday morning we called up a ship but nothing else much happened a great deal of talking is carried on about home. Saturday noon we altered course off Galite Island. During the afternoon I did the last of the Light Lists. Sunday morning I kept a lookout most of the night. The wind was Northerly and a bit chilly. Sunday afternoon we passed Algiers and we saw quite a few ships.

The weather was quite warm Monday morning the temperature was again down. During the afternoon we passed 'Gib' we were abeam at 1457 and although we were eight miles off they still called us up. At 1600 we had just altered off Cape Tarifa and were on 270 degrees. I stayed on the bridge until 1630 as the D.F. was being calibrated and I might have been required for the wheel. At midnight we were approaching Vincent and we altered about 0345. We were on bearings during the afternoon and even though there is a long swell we are still doing 16.04 knots. Midnight found us looking for Finisterre and we altered off Cape Canon at 0410. We were now in the bay but the weather is still pretty good. All day it was overcast and force 7/8 winds. But at 1600 the sun was out and we got a sight. We sighted Ushant at 0245 Thursday morning after looking for it for over an hour. It rose just for'ard of the beam. We altered course, on to 51 degrees, up the channel at 0400.

The weather is really cold now the temperature at 0400 being 49 degrees. We were all turned to on daywork during our watches scrubbing the wheelhouse and cleaning brass. During the afternoon I cleaned the remaining brass on the Bridge and then helped John, Bob, and Bareta scrape paint spots off the boat deck. During the evening I squared up my office work. When I went on watch we were just approaching Folkestone. I made twelve pots of tea during the watch as well as a few cups of coffee we anchored off Sea Reach #2 at 0406. We hove up at 0830 and we were at Gravesend at 1005 where we change Pilots. I relieved Ian on the bridge. We were off the locks at 1140. All fast in the locks at 1203. We left the locks at 1230 and were all fast by 1324.

What We Learnt…

As P. J. Wood started this voyage as a Senior Midshipman he had to almost immediately step up and show some leadership by keeping him and the other Middies, two of whom were first-trippers, spirits up as they left Birkenhead. There was a lot more than just cleaning, painting and watching cargo on this voyage, office work and logs were the order of the day and cargo plans all of which improved his seamanship skills over the voyage.

One of the main differences between this and the previous voyages is that there were a number of films shown, this was due to Clytoneus having passengers on board. I think we can all agree the reviews, when he could be bothered to mention them in the log, were short, to the point and in general lined up quite closely with the IMDB reviews and scores.

This trip was not all films and cargo plans though, there was also drama on the high seas; two fires to deal with, one of which was reported in the log in a rather blasé manner of lobbing the bucket in question over the side. There was enough risk of pirates, that patrols were common throughout the voyage.

While the long hours and work did not change, the Middies on the halfdeck did decide to live it up a bit and add to the urban myth of POSH standing for Port Out, Starboard Home – by putting their tables and chairs out on the port side to work and relax after the day's chores.

There was further birthday disappointment for P. J. Wood, his third birthday on board, when his plans to go ashore got canned by the Mate and then when they decided to invite some of the engineers to the Halfdeck for a little celebration, he was then informed that no one apart from the Middies were allowed there – I am wondering if he did send his complaint into the union?

"…so we have to sit in this abhorrent little festering set of

uninsulated bulkheads just because people misinterpret some bloody archaic set papers we signed before we knew better."

Was it all bad? No, there were mountain trips, a DJ set, a Christmas spent in Trincomalee (Sri Lanka) and as the Senior Midshipman, when they acquired a new Middy in Belwan, he got a single berth cabin after a little over 3 years at sea.

For Christmas, it seems that P. J. Wood is a creature of habit or at least has continued the tradition of eating well in the morning, having naps and then eating some more – that is at least how I remember my childhood Christmas days!

M.V. AUTOMEDON

June 1964
Voy. 38

Master:	W. J. S. Eynon
Mate:	D. W. MacDonald
2nd Mate:	W. Fleming
3rd Mate:	G. L. Harcombe
4th Mate:	J. P. Jones

<u>Cadet Officers</u>
- J. A. Millar
- P. J. Wood

"Your course of training during the apprenticeship will offer numerous opportunities to improve your skill, knowledge and ability. Take every opportunity that offers and make the most of them."

- *Midshipman Appointment Letter from Alfred Holt & Co. circa 1960*

Voyage of M.V. Automedon - Map

Voyage Statistics

Monday 1st June 1964 - Birkenhead - Joined Ship

Wednesday 10th June - Port Said

Suez Canal Transit

Monday 15th June 1964 - Aden

Thursday 25th June 1964 - Penang

Friday 26th of June 1964 - Port Swettenham (Port Klang)

Tuesday 30th June 1964 - Singapore

Wednesday 8th July 1964 - Hong Kong

Monday 13th July 1964 - Shanghai

Sunday 19th July 1964 - Hsinkang

Tuesday 4th August 1964 - Yokohama

Tuesday 11th August 1964 - Hong Kong

Thursday 20th August 1964 - Singapore

Sunday 23rd August 1964 - Port Swettenham (Port Klang)

Tuesday 25th August 1964 - Penang

Thursday 3rd September 1964 - Aden

Monday 7th September 1964 - Suez

Suez Canal Transit

Wednesday 9th September 1964 - Port Said

Thursday 17th September 1964 – Liverpool

Total number of Ports visited: 18

Total Voyage time: 108 days
Total Voyage Distance*: 24,775 Nautical miles

* All distances are estimated using Reed's New Maritime Distance Tables (1965) [Acquired from Fenton Steamship Co. Chartering and S&P department] and by going "old school" with Lloyds Atlas of World Shipping Ports (30th Edition). Ports, wharfs, jetties and buoys have all changed dramatically over the last 62 years so that calculating accurate distances is nearly impossible to determine, so we used our best judgement.

Birkenhead.

Monday 1st June 1964.

John Millar and I were to sail on the "*Automedon*" this trip and we joined lunchtime of sailing day. We then went to sign on but all the E.D.'s were out to lunch when we arrived at the Mercantile Marine Office so our journey was in vain. We returned to the ship for inspection at 1430 when we stood on the prom deck checking the rooms. At 1600 there was a boat drill after which we started unpacking. We stayed onboard until about 1900 waiting to hear about signing on and then gave up and met John Peterson. For stand-by one of us was on the wheel and I was on the gangway. Stand-by was at 2330 and we moved to the locks. We were all fast by 0030 when we were to await the tide.

Birkenhead – Port Said.

Tuesday 2nd June – Wednesday 10th June.

At 0245 stand-by went for moving out of the locks and I made the pilot ladder up and turned to for a short while before the 4-8. There was to be a cadet officer and two Mates on each watch. At 0417 we were abeam of the "*Bar Lightvessel*[45]" and at 0730 we rounded The Skerries. The Pilot was away at 0751 and F.S.A. was 0800. The weather has been really dismal with rain and reduced visibility and the 12-4 that afternoon was no exception. We altered course to 199+1 degrees off The Smalls at about 1500. We worked the dog watches and I did the 6-8. At midnight double watches finished so for this week I will be on the 12-4. During the watch I worked out an error and had to put it in the ship's deviation book. At 0400 we were just entering the bay. During the afternoon watch we again encountered heavy rain. The wind was about force 6 for most of the watch. Thursday morning we were not bothered so much by the rain but the sea was rough and we were taking light water for'd. At 0336 we altered off Finisterre to 171+2 degrees. By the afternoon the weather had improved immensely, but there was still a moderate swell. Noon was at 1338 and as yet I haven't got everything taped up as I had last trip. We have started taking the Double Bottom oil temperatures under #3 where some condensed milk is stowed.

Friday morning there was quite a bit of traffic and I put her down a few times and answered a Norwegian ship which called us up. At 0400 we were three miles from the alter course position of Cape St. Vincent. When I went on watch at noon, we were about 30 miles from the alter course position off Cape Trafalgar. There was a lot of traffic about, including four Spanish frigates which didn't have the courtesy to answer our dips. We altered off Spartel about 1445 and at 1600 we were a beam of 'Gib'. They didn't call us up though. It has been very warm all day, though not unpleasantly hot.

Saturday morning there was no wind at all and very little cloud it was quite chilly though and that was pleasant. We altered course to 082 degrees at 0115 and for the remainder of the watch Cabo de Gata was in sight. When I went on watch at noon we were on bearings with the North Coast of Africa. There wasn't much traffic and the temperature was well up in the seventies and all in all it was a very pleasant watch.

Sunday morning we picked up Cape Bougaroun about 0230 by radar and 0400 we were nearly abeam of it. Today we change watches and I go onto the 8-12. I shall do both 12-4's and the evening 8-12. During the mornings I cleaned the place up which doesn't entail very much than read and write letters etc. We aren't off watch together very much but otherwise I'm settling down to the trip quite well I think.

During the afternoon watch there was quite a lot of traffic and visibility was not too good. The weather was much warmer and we will soon be in whites. At 2000 I went on watch again and we were in bearings with Pantellaria. Two ships called us up and very soon it was midnight. Monday morning I was woken by the whistle at about ten to seven. We were in fog. It had cleared up by the time I went on watch, but it was still misty. I took a sight and worked it up to noon and then at 1030 the fog suddenly appeared again and we reduced. I had to blow the whistle. But we were out of it again by 1115. Noon was at 1153. We passed very few ships during the evening and the clocks were advanced one hour, making the watch pass quickly. It was quite chilly and cardigans were the order of the day by 2200.

Tuesday morning most of my watch was spent keeping a lookout and working up my sight. The temperature was 78 degrees Fahrenheit but felt colder. During the afternoon I did some dhobi, wrote letters and log. The evening watch was shorter again by half an hour and we only saw two ships the whole watch.

Wednesday morning we passed *"Diomed*[46]*"* and after taking the sight nothing particularly happened. When I went on Watch It 2000 we were approaching Port Said. We anchored at 2048 and then waited knowing we wouldn't go in before 2300. At 2315 we had word over the VHF to be ready to heave away and we immediately tested the gear. At midnight stand-by went.

Port Said.
Canal Transit.
Thursday 11th June – Friday 12th June.

I was on the pilot ladder and gangway for stand-by and very longwinded everything appeared to be. We were all fast though by 0200 when I turned in. Next morning we were called at 0700 to test gear and I went aft. John stayed on the bridge until after breakfast when I relieved him. We singled up immediately. We let go at 0824 and we entered the canal itself at 0836. I just kept the movement book and put her down on the chart but the watch passed reasonably quickly and at 1145 we entered the cut. We were all fast by 1215. During the afternoon, several of us went for a swim which was refreshing even in that water. We were still in the cut when I went on watch at 2000. At about 2015 the *"Atreus*[47]*"* past us Northbound and at 2040 the *"Tantalus"* past. The last ship cleared the end of the cut at about 2100 and by 2120 we were underway again. We changed Pilots at 2242 and at midnight we were just entering the Bitter Lakes. We were clear of the canal by 0345 Friday. F.S.A. was at 0418.

Suez – Aden.
Friday 12th June – Monday 15th June.

When I went on watch at 0800 we were only about halfway down Suez Bay with quite a bit of traffic. We were on the alter course off Ras Ghareb at 1028 and abeam of the same place on the new course at 1042. For a while a self-propelled oil rig had us guessing but other than that, everything was straightforward. The weather was much warmer with worse, we fear, to come. Most of the afternoon was spent keeping cool. During the evening watch we experienced some super refraction, visually, as well as on the radar. The Brothers were abeam at 2023 and we could still see their light at about 2315. On the radar we picked up some land at 7.5 miles and 8.5 miles. The nearest land was in actually 39 miles away.

Saturday morning the heat was HOT. I was very glad when the watch came to an end. Noon was at 1230 which John took. During the afternoon I went for a swim and then bought my log up to date. During the evening watch nothing of note happened. The only two ships we saw all watch were never nearer than five miles. At midnight though, four ships suddenly appeared ahead. The temperature was 85 degrees all watch.

Sunday again, linen change and watch change. I did the 8-12 in the morning and although it was a shade cooler it was still unpleasant. Noon was at 1218. I was off then until midnight. During the afternoon, I went for a swim and sunbathed. During the evening I started a letter home.

Monday morning when I went on watch, we were expecting to pick up the light from of Hells Gates about 0100. We saw it first at 0115 and we altered course off the light at 0242. At 0400 the light was only just visible astern. About 0900 we altered course off Perim and at noon we were about 45 miles from the Fairway buoy. We picked up the Pilot at 1255, about a mile outside the port limits. We went alongside one of the new permanent refuelling berths and we were all fast by 1609.

Aden.
Monday 15th June.
No cargo had to be worked, so John and I divided our efforts to buying a pair of binoculars. Which eventually bought after about an hour. On watch we now have a new toy. We decided against going ashore when we found we had to be back for chow. During the evening we read and discussed our letters. At 2000 I made a gallant effort at turning in. I was called at 2215 to go on the gangway and after putting the pilot ladder over we had difficulty raising the gangway as the winch didn't work. We made a lead item though to #15 winch on the sailors house. Full away was before midnight.

Aden – Penang.
Tuesday 16th June – Thursday 25th June.
I felt well equipped with my 'binocs' but unfortunately there wasn't much to look at. At 0045 the gyro passed out and we started steering by magnetic compass on the wheel. Other than this, the watch passed slowly, humidly and uneventfully.

I woke up Tuesday morning feeling very hot and uncomfortable. By noon the heat was really hitting us and we had a force 4 wind astern, giving us really a flat calm onboard. During the afternoon the temperature reached 111 degrees on the port wing and 103 on the starboard wing. At 1700 whilst I was reading on the aft end of the boat deck, the engine room telegraphs clanged and we altered course to port. We then saw a native dhow with 15 chaps aboard attracting our attention. When they were alongside everybody was out with their cameras and new Aden binoculars anxious not to miss anything. No one on the dhow could speak English but they soon made it clear that they wanted water. They filled their two 50-gallon drums and several other containers whilst they also asked for food and cigarettes. Being very generous about half a dozen old loaves were dropped to them and about 30 cigarettes, all of which were collected by one chap, probably the fellow to be voted "Most likely to succeed" by his classmates. By various other means, we found out they wanted Razazier, so we indicated South and then continued on our weary way.

Wednesday mornings watch was much cooler, verging on cold and I put on a sweater at smoko. There was a heavy southeasterly swell and the wind had shifted to a couple of points for'ard of the beam. We sighted no ships at all and the watch past uneventfully. Wednesday midday we were north of Socotra but at 1300 we were out of its lee and steering 105 degrees. We were rolling heavily and at 1540 we did three or four really big rolls which caused great havoc. At 1600 the Captain took charge and we steered 035 degrees until 1800 we gradually came back to 105. At 1600, the gyro failed just to add to the confusion.

Thursday morning, we were still rolling heavily and we called up a ship to ask what weather she had experienced, unfortunately after exchanging names we came to a 'checkmate'. Subsequently the weather eased off a little and now in the middle of the morning, we were rolling only moderately. It was warm again in the afternoon and I spent quite a while ruling up two new slates. We saw one ship only during the whole watch.

Friday morning, the clocks were advanced another 30 minutes, putting us four and half hours ahead of GMT. As I had not slept well before the watch I was very tired until between two and four I managed to wake up of course. I saw only two ships during the watch. The afternoon watch passed quickly and I did some work for the Second Mate. After smoko I took a sight so that kept me occupied until one bell when I gave the usual calls. We had boat drill and fire drill at 1615 but as we were rolling the boats were not swung out.

Saturday mornings watch was very quiet as we only saw one ship. There was a little rain about but it did not affect us. I took an error at 0330, but otherwise I just kept a lookout. We had an Engine room fire drill at 0930 which caught me unawares whilst I was taking the oil temperatures. Just afterwards we had a heavy shower of rain otherwise the weather is very pleasant now.

Sunday morning I kept a lookout and we sighted only two ships. I took an error and after giving the one bell calls I turned in feeling once again that I had done a good job as lookout. The afternoon was quite pleasant, but nothing of note happened. We changed watches today and I went on the 8-12 in the evening.

Monday morning I took a sight and kept a lookout during the evening watch we left the bearings of Ceylon on the last lap to Sumatra.

Tuesday morning a ship, which must have been doing exactly the same speed as us, was still just abaft our starboard beam. At noon we were a little south of the line and our companion crossed astern and went about two miles north of us. Midnight Tuesday we had not sighted Sumatra.

Wednesday at 0800 we were on bearings though they were not too clear. At noon we were still on bearings with Diamond Head and by this time the swell of the monsoon had completely died away. At 2000 that evening we were keeping good lookout for Penang Island Light. At about 2130 we sighted it. We had a fairly steady drizzle and several knots of fishing boats so a good lookout had to be kept. At 2200, the clocks were advanced an hour. At 0015 the Pilot was on board with the long-anticipated mail. I turned in after reading mine. I was not called again until 0600 when we heaved up to go alongside. We were all fast by 0830 with a shore gangway. I was on cargo until noon and we were working sixes.

Penang.
Thursday 25th June – Friday 26th June.

I went ashore during the afternoon and managed to spend $20 in about two hours. I returned to the ship for a snooze and after chow went on deck again. We had to make notes of any damage caused by bad loading and this was easy enough to do. At midnight, John came on and as we were to sail at 0300, I got my head down quickly. Surprisingly, I was not called for stand-by, so the next I knew it was 0700.

Penang – Port Swettenham.
Friday 26th of June.
During the morning 8-12 I actually put down some bearings and we had altered course about 0930. During the rest of the watch I kept the usual lookout. We arrived at the Pilot at 1500. We then proceeded to the new wharf where we immediately went alongside and we were all fast by 1730.

Port Swettenham.
Friday 26th June – Monday 29th June.
During the first evening only one of us was required to stand-by and this was me as John is to do the night. At 2100 I was needed to unlock all the cars in #3 aft deep tank. By 2230 about four had been unloaded and the gangs knocked off.

I was on Saturday morning again, so I was down the tank again for about five hours until the cars finished. After that I toured all the hatches looking for damaged cargo to put in my little red book. I went ashore Saturday afternoon for a swim and became very dejected in the swimming pool as I had gone ashore on my own. At 1600 our football team turned up and we played the "*Memnon*[48]". I returned to the ship for chow and then turned in for the night. We had to turn the gangway out about 0230 as previously we had been below the level of the wharf otherwise very little happened.

I was on Sunday afternoon and watched cars being discharged from #5 at a great rate of knots. We had a little interest when at about 1500 twenty or so young women came on board wanting to see over the ship. The Mate couldn't allow it as cargo was working, but there were plenty of volunteers to show them the accommodation. I was off Sunday evening, so I went to the movie at the Mission.

Monday morning, only two hatches were working #3 and #5. At about 1000 a friend came aboard from the "*Glenartney*[49]" but otherwise nothing particular happened. At 1200 I went down to the "*Glenartney*" for a tour. We tested gear at 1500 and left at 1600. I was on the bridge for stand-by and was at the wheel for at least half a mile. I stayed on the bridge until the Pilot was away at 1715. We passed over a bar with only five feet beneath us.

Port Swettenham – Singapore.
Monday 27th June – Tuesday 30th June.
At 2000 we were abeam of Port Dickson. During the watch I put her down at quarter to and quarter past the hour. I was called again at 0540 to go on the bridge. When I got up at 0550 we were going dead slow ahead which we were on until 0642. We anchored at 0648 to await the Pilot.

Singapore.
Tuesday 30th June – Saturday 4th July.
The Pilot was on board at 0650 and at 0705 we commenced to weigh anchor. The anchor was away at 0715. We proceeded in but had to wait for our entry signal which was not hoisted until 0725. We went alongside. Godowns 10/11 and I took the wheel about half a cable from the berth, really skilled! We worked the same hours here as in Swettenham, one of us on during the day until 1700 and then one on the night. I was on until noon when John came on. I went ashore during the afternoon and did a lot of shopping. We had chow in the Cellar and returned to the ship about 1900 to turn in for the night. John was just off ashore when I returned, it's a great pity we can't get ashore together once in a while.

Wednesday morning, nothing happened and the night passed uneventfully. Wednesday afternoon, cargo continued without much ado. I watched and tallied specials from #5 lockers until 1600, after which I carried on as normal. Thursday night was done by John and during the evening I went ashore and met Fred Puntain off the "*Rhexenor*[50]" I returned to the ship about 10 o'clock as we were to sail at six Saturday morning.

Singapore – Hong Kong.
Saturday 4th July – Wednesday 8th July.

John went on the bridge for stand-by and we were clear of the wharf by 0630 as the Pilot was leaving by the gangway, I had very little to do. We left via the western roads and past the old "*Gorgon*[51]", now Hong Kong III, which had been arrested. The Pilot left at 0715. I went on the bridge at 0800 and during the morning we calibrated the D.F. or rather, tried to. During this watch I put her down for the Captain and altered course for Pestanama. We stayed on our watches for the whole of the trip to Hong Kong and during the evening watch a good lookout had to be kept for fishermen and junks.

Midnight Tuesday, we could see the glow of Victoria Island on the horizon. I was called again at 0540 and went on the bridge immediately. We were about two miles from Lei Mun Pass [Lei Yue Mun] at 0600 and at 0610 the Pilot was onboard. We anchored for quarantine and immigration at 0630 and we proceeded in at 0715. We were all fast at Holt's Wharf by 0830 with "*Glenartney*" astern of us.

Hong Kong.
Wednesday 8th July – Saturday 11th July.
At 0915 the crashing blow fell, we were to work sixes, and I was on the 12-6. It was, as usual, difficult to get on deck at first because of the tailors and the laundry people, which kept demanding my valuable time. When I did make it, I was kept busy checking beam bolts and searching for special cargo which was 'mislaid'. When John came on at 12 all hatches were working smoothly with eleven gangs. During the afternoon I went ashore and did a great deal of shopping with the 4th Mate. We were back aboard by six and we were both on the evening. At eleven the gangs knocked off, and as only three or four gangs were to work the night, John was not required so the sixes won't be too bad.

I didn't go ashore Thursday morning, but I went to see Jerry and Pete on the "Glenartney". During the afternoon we were not very busy although all hatches were working. During the evening I went ashore just to do a little shopping. I returned to the ship at 2355 after meeting Jerry and Pete ashore. I, luckily, was not required so I turned in until 0530 when the 4th Mate called me to take over. Unfortunately for him we had to test the wells in #3 for'ard deep tanks so he had to stay up. Nothing happened of note during Friday mornings watch after we had successfully pumped the wells in the deep tank. #6 finished about 0900 and was then cleaned ready for painting. Only three hatches were working that evening of which I was glad because I had a hard afternoon tracking round Hong Kong trying to find out how to be issued with a visa to get to Macau, which John and I want to do homeward bound.

Saturday morning I didn't go ashore but wrote letters and at noon when I went on we had almost finished cargo. We tested the gear at 1730 and sailed at 1830. I was on the bridge for stand-by and full speed away was rung at 2000.

Hong Kong – Shanghai.
Saturday 11th July – Monday 13th July.
Sunday morning we were on bearings with China and we saw quite a few junks. The clocks were retarded 30 minutes at midnight and by 0400 we were just entering the Taiwan Strait. During the afternoon it was warm and a good lookout had to be kept for junks. At 1500 we were 'buzzed' by a US naval plane, but otherwise nothing of note happened. Monday we didn't sight land, though during the afternoon we had the radar on from 1400 as a check. By 1700 the water was a dirty colour and we knew that the Yangtze was near. At midnight I went on the bridge we were in the Yangtze approaching Woosung where we anchored at 0030.

Shanghai.
Tuesday 14th July – Friday 17th July.
As soon as we anchored, I had to ask the shore station how long till quarantine? My effort did not particularly enhance my reputation as a signalman, but next time I shall feel more at ease with it. We had the muster almost immediately after which

I went round with the official lavatory attendant? quarantine officer! Locking, or otherwise effectively sealing all the W.C.'s. At 0530 I went on the bridge for stand-by and we were just entering the Shanghai Wanshoo. I put her down and kept the movement book until 0730 when we were just off buoys #33, when I took the wheel. We were all fast by 0800 and already the heat was oppressive and the atmosphere of Shanghai making great inroads into our healthy chests. We would not work cargo until we went alongside, so John and I were on the nights. During that afternoon, we watched the great volume of traffic on the river the bulk of which were very fine sailing junks. We split the night between us and I did the 11-3.

Wednesday afternoon, John and I went ashore to the Seaman's Club and Friendship Store. I could have spent a fortune on carpets had I the money, but instead I bought a thick coat. We moved alongside at 2000 and were all fast by 2230. Much to our surprise, we were not required until 0800 Thursday. I was on the 12-4 and by noon discharging was nearly complete. We loaded in numbers #1, #2 and #5 that afternoon and I spent most of my time in #2. The gangs were greatly molly coddled having fans in the hatches keeping a good, forced draught going which was extremely pleasant. As the temperature was well over a hundred, they were worthwhile.

At midnight I went to #5 starboard locker and made sure that they blocked up with bales of hair. Then to #1. O.D. to supervise the dunnaging prior to loading cans of fish. Drums were to be loaded into #5 port locker so I spent full half an hour removing the bottom dog on the sea door. Cargo finished at 1000.

The muster was at 1300 and at 1400 we tested the gear. 1415 we commenced singling up and I was on the wheel. First we had to move upriver to swing which took quite a while as the tug could not make the line fast. I was relieved of the wheel at 1525 and I then realised how hot it had been, 110 degrees since noon. I stood by the gangway until the first Pilot left at Woosung at 1725. We then headed down the Yangtze and away from the heat and the smell of Shanghai. The Pilot was away at 1930.

Shanghai to Hsinkang
Friday 17th July – Sunday 19th July.

When I went on watch at midnight there were no ships and the sky was overcast, so I was unable to take an error. During the afternoon we saw several Japanese fishing boats and at 1530 I took a sight. Sunday morning there were several junks and by 0200 we were on bearings. At 0400 we were five miles from the alter course and, thankfully, the signal station. We were on bearings for noon and at 1306 we reduced speed. We were anchored by 1324 and we then had the Inspection until 1430.

Hsinkang
Sunday 19th July – Thursday 30th July.

After the inspection, we were told we would be anchored for at least a week, so the Mate put us on daywork. There were then nine ships ahead of us.

Monday morning we were called at 0700 and after breakfast and taking the temperatures I washed the deckhead in the halfdeck and then scraped around the rusty rivets. John did another test during the morning and in the afternoon we started painting the deckhead. It was a great luxury to have all night off and I started making a calendar that I've wanted to do all voyage.

Tuesday morning we finished the dayroom deckhead, we are a little out of practise and the result is barely satisfactory, and then I started the bathroom. The deckheads were finished by 1500, so I then started on the bulkheads with John. During the evening, I continued with my calendar and turned in early.

Wednesday we finished the bulkheads by 1400 and the cutting in was complete by 1500. After smoko we gave the halfdeck good clean out. I finished my calendar during the evening and did some reading. At about 2200 we were infested with swarms of beetles and hardly a step could be taken outside without crunching one.

The first job Thursday was to clear away all of the beetles

as they burrow into any rotten wood, paint or pitch they can find. John and I went around with flit guns spraying anywhere they could hide. After smoko I cleaned out the boat deck locker, suggied and scraped it before lunch. Afterwards I put on some quick drying red lead and started painting it. The locker was completely finished by 1715. We were now first ship in the queue of five, but at 2000 one of the latest arrivals went inside, much to everyone's disgust.

Friday, after cleaning out the halfdeck I checked the hoses and nozzles. During the afternoon we did some study. We had boat and fire drill at 1615.

Saturday we did a few odd jobs and after smoko replaced the traveller on the sounding boom. We had the afternoon off, during which I did some dhobi.

Sunday was an anniversary, eight weeks ago I said my fond farewells and it was the halfway date of the scheduled voyage and we have been anchored here a week. There weren't any celebrations. During the afternoon we did some bronzying and then joined in a water fight with the sailors. All good clean fun. We went on to sea watches at 2000 and I went on the 8 to 12. We tested gear at 2315 and to everyone's surprise, we moved in at 0030 after being anchored for seven and a half days. We were alongside by 0300, but no cargo was due to start until 0800.

Yes, you guessed correctly, it was raining at 0800 and no cargo was worked until 1100 when 72 drums of gasoline were taken off the deck at #5. By 1300 it was raining again and we went on to sixes. Monday afternoon and evening the rain continued so no work was done.

Tuesday's 6-12 was also wet but only spitting this time; again I just stood by in the halfdeck doing one or two odd jobs. The afternoon saw the weather clear up but still no sign of any gangs. I went ashore and posted a letter and returned to the ship for chow. During the evening we were expecting gangs to turn up from 1600. Eventually one gang arrived for #2 at 2200. By 2300 the tween deck had been discharged but lower hold was not started until after midnight, when we had two gangs.

At 0600 Wednesday #2 and #4 were working, I stood by until chow time and then relieved the 4th Mate. After my chow I cleaned #2 aft well and then the gangs knocked off again. We had plenty of work during the evening, up until 2000 I was doing a chalk separation in #2 tween decks. Then after that I supervised the dunnage laying in #2 lower hold. By 2200 the gang had the idea and I had a smoke. Some oil was being transferred from #4 port to #3 starboard to bring the ship upright and I was taking the ullages until Chippy took over at 2300. At midnight we changed gangs and five started work.

Thursday morning we had five gangs and worked all hatches. Until chow I was separating in #2 T.D., after which I relieve 2nd Sparks who was tallying specials in the strong room. By 1000 the options had finished in #2, so I then went to #6 D.T. By midday we had nearly finished cargo. We tested gear at 1400 and when stand-by went at 1500 people were surprised as we had expected the muster first. We were clear of the wharf by 1545, after waiting for the tug and then for the dredger, when we headed for Taku Bar for the muster. We anchored at Taku at 1730 and had the muster immediately, which only lasted half an hour. At 1800 moved about half a mile and anchored again, this time for engine repairs. These took until 1900 when we got underway again and at last headed for ----? We are not sure whether it's Yoko or Hong Kong.

Hsinkang to Yokohama?
Thursday 30th July – Tuesday 4th August.
Everyone was relieved to be away from Hsinkang but it was not nearly as bad as any Java ports, apart that is, from the organisation. I am on the 8-12 and when I went on watch at 2000 we were all clear of land but not fishermen. We altered course at 2306 onto 107 degrees. We passed the Chang Shan I signal station before 0400 Friday and by 0800 we were 40 miles from the corner of the Province of Shanting. At 0934 we ran into fog and were reduced until 1142. My job was to keep the whistle going and write up the movement book. During the

afternoon, we ran into heavy rain for a while. The weather is not expected to improve either as we are approaching typhoon Hela. If she recurves it won't be too bad, if not we will have to alter course. At the moment we are heading in the general direction of Yokohama. The evenings watched past with the sighting of only one ship. We altered course 157 degrees at about 2240.

Saturday morning we ran it into fog at 0512 which was clear by 0800. The visibility was perfect by 1100. Noon was at 1150. During the afternoon we altered onto 207 degrees. At about 1800 however we altered on to 102 degrees. The weather has been, as stated, foggy but the sea has been smooth with a low westerly swell. The evenings watch passed uneventfully but we sighted a lot of fishermen. Sunday morning was quite warm but the watch passed without incident. The evenings watch was better as we were on bearings.

Monday morning, we picked up land just about 10 minutes before apparent noon, so we didn't take a sight. The evening 8-12 started off quietly enough but by 2100 when we hadn't sighted the light we were looking for, things didn't look too bright. About 2130 we were amongst a lot of very bright phosphorescence, which made keeping a lookout difficult. At 2230 a beam of light had been spotted by me and unfortunately only me, then at 2245 we ran into fog. I kept the whistle going, except when I was sent off on odd jobs including bringing in the log. Just before midnight the light we had been looking for appeared on the port beam. We were out of the fog then until 0100.

I was called at 0550 to go onto the bridge and as soon as I arrived the 4th Mate went for'ard for anchoring. We anchored to await quarantine at 0636. At 0715 we were on our way in again. We were all fast by 0815.

Yokohama.
Tuesday 4th August – Thursday 6th August.
At first, the Mate wanted one on to watch #4 port and starboard deep tanks which were to be pressure tested. These we

filled by 1300 and then went on to sixes again, 'just until things ease off a bit'. As only two gangs were working, we realised that it would be for the duration of our stay. During the afternoon I went ashore and did some shopping. During the evening we worked 3 gangs in two hatches, 4A and #5. By midnight the best part of each side of the tunnel was full.

Wednesday, John went to Tokyo so I did the 0600-1830. During the morning there was nothing to do, but I spent the afternoon on deep tanks. Firstly I cleaned and tested #3 deep tank well, which took some doing as both stern boxes were full of congealed palm oil. When that was completed, #4 starboard was being pumped into #3 starboard. This was finished by 1730. When John returned from Tokyo he'd had a good day as well. During the evening I went ashore. I went on at 0600, but no cargo started until 0800. There were 61 tons remaining, all for #2. Some was transshipment though which went into the tween deck. Cargo finished at 1130. We sailed at 1230 and I was on the gangway for stand-by. Feeling very cobby as I couldn't find my seaman's card with my pass and about ¥2000. It was not so much the fact of losing the card and the money, as the stupidity of doing it.

British Seaman's card

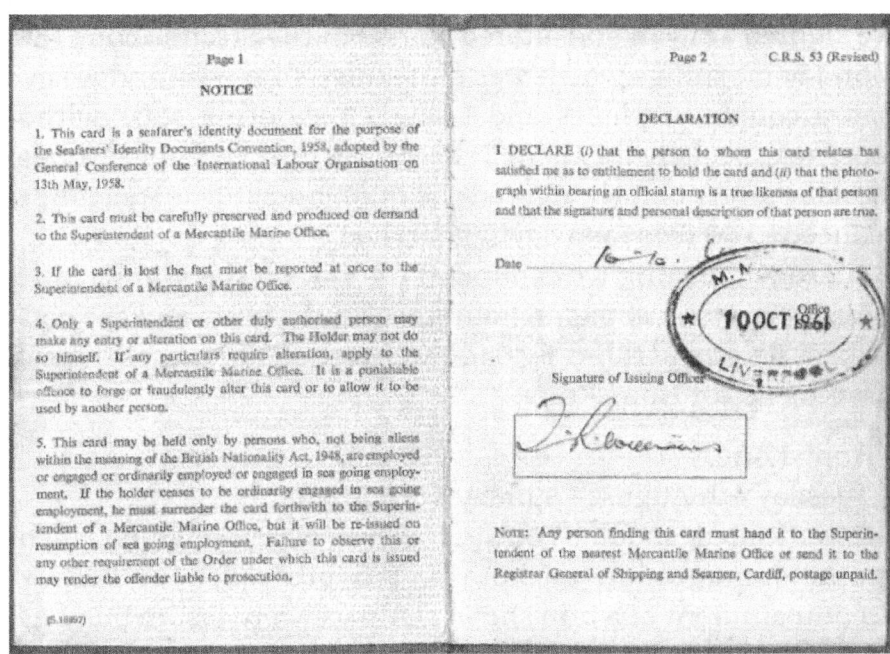

Yokohama to Hong Kong.

Thursday 6th August – Tuesday 11th August.

The Pilot was away at 1800 and I'm on the 12-4 for this run. I relieve John at 1430 after falling asleep in the bath. By then we were clear of Yokohama Bay. Friday mornings Watch was quiet until 0230 when we ran into rain. I spent the remainder of the watch watching the radar but we didn't sight any ships. Friday afternoon, we were on bearings for a while, but we didn't sight any other ships. I found my seaman's card and money, which was a great relief.

Saturday morning we sighted a lot of fishermen and two ships. We are pitching moderately and the lookout was posted on the monkey island. Saturday noon we were on bearings with Otake Shima and by 1400 we had sighted Iowa Shima which is supposed to be an active volcano. It looked very dead to us. The 3rd Mate was taken ill during the day and when I went on the bridge at midnight the Captain had done that 8-12. The weather is still moderate and overcast.

The mornings watch passed uneventfully. Sunday afternoon

we sighted Taiwan and altered course in the Straits about 1800. Monday mornings watch was quite busy ship wise and we even had a couple of planes and I saw 27 shooting stars without looking especially for them. It keeps the mind occupied though. Monday afternoon we sighted the mainland and at star time we reduced to 60 revs for a daylight arrival.

Tuesday morning we calibrated the D.F. on the Wang Lum Lt. House. This took about an hour and a half as a careful eye had to be kept on other traffic. By 0400 we were steaming south before heading up for Hong Kong.

Hong Kong.
Tuesday 4th August – Sunday 16th August.

I was called about 0700 just as we were weighing anchor in the immigration anchorage. We proceeded in with the accompaniment of a rain shower, and we were fast to buoy A12, just outside the Macao harbour limits judging by the distance steamed by 0815. After breakfast we were told we could go ashore for the day, so by the time the launch was alongside we were ready to go. Our first job ashore was to make sure we had no friends on either the "*Clytoneus*" or the "*Breckonshire*[52]". We knew all the Middies, but not well, so we started our 1000 spending spree. By 2200 we were just about tired out, but as one had to be on the night we had to return to the ship. I did the night and nothing untoward happened. At noon I was on again and we were working two gangs. We loaded some specials into #1, but otherwise all was quiet. I went ashore that evening and met John, who was to do the night

Thursday we went on to sixes, which was a bit annoying, but there were more gangs so things began to happen. I was on the 'favourite' 6-12 watch and Thursday evening I kept quite busy. Friday afternoon I went ashore again and when I returned, I counted 68 Junks alongside, I can think of only one anomaly which I won't bother to mention here. During the evening, many of these lighters were dispatched, but the one holding everything up was one loading into #3 starboard deep tank.

We had 200 tons of bulk Barytes which gave the appearance of chipped marble and is used in plate glass manufacturer, as a colouring agent and a chemical reagent. The cargo was held up periodically by rain showers and we did not sail until Sunday lunchtime, in the rain of course.

Hong Kong – Singapore.
Sunday 16th August – Thursday 20th August

I was on the 8 -12 for this trip and for the first two days we had quite rough weather. There was quite a bit of traffic all the way. Tuesday midnight I turned in and dropped quickly to sleep when all of a sudden I woke up with a terrible din engulfing me. I found I was standing dressed, trying to figure out what I was doing then I realised the fire alarm was ringing. How I dressed without waking up, I'll never know. Anyway, I went aft to the tunnel escape where I regulated the opening and closing of the door and stood by the telephone. After five minutes we were asked to open the door as the firefighters couldn't breathe. By 0350 the fire was out and by 0400 I was asleep again.

Wednesday evenings watch was eventful, at 2100 we stopped engines so that the engineers could work on them and a Shell tanker going the same way as us struck up a 'conversation' with us and I spent an hour practising with a Middy on her, after we got going again. Thursday morning, we were on bearings and we sighted Horsburgh lighthouse about 1130. We anchored in the roads at about 1530.

Singapore.
Thursday 20th August – Saturday 22nd August.

At 1630 I went on the bridge to keep the wheel turned and at 1700 we hove up to go alongside. I was on the gangway and we were all fast by 1815. I was on deck during the evening and we worked five gangs mainly discharging coast cargo and shifting home cargo. John did the night and I was on the following morning watching in #1 strong room. During the afternoon I went ashore to Connell House for a swim until about 1500 when

I went on into the town and to do some shopping. I met John at 1845 and we went to see "The Manchurian Candidate", which was very good.

I was on the 11-7 and as we returned the "*William Rays*[53]" was sailing from the berth astern of us. During the night nothing happened, and when I came on again at noon cargo had just about finished. I was on the gangway for stand-by and we were clear by 1730.

Singapore – Swettenham and Penang.
Saturday 22nd August – Tuesday 25th August.

I went on the 12-4 and we had quite a busy watch with plenty of ships. We overtook the "*Naya*[54]" which was supposed to be racing us for a berth, about 0230 and at 0500 the Pilot was aboard. We went straight alongside, Sunday morning, and I was on cargo. We were loading rubber into #3 and #4 only and by noon had got on quite well. I was to do the night but didn't go ashore until about 1600. I met John ashore later and after doing some shopping we watched "The Last Voyage", the Sunday night film at the Seaman's Club.

The night was quiet and at noon when I went on cargo, I had to watch the fore peak tank being topped up with fresh water for a pressure test. When that was over, I was down #1 and supervised the shifting of cartons of pineapple to make space. We sailed at 1500 and when I had showered, I relieved John on the bridge. Full speed away was 1630.

Tuesday morning was quite busy again and at 0400 we were about 16 miles from the Pilot. We anchored at about 0700 and one was required. John stayed on and I wrote letters. Cargo was finished at 1400. The ship was completely full. We sailed immediately and I was on the bridge again for stand-by.

Penang – Aden.
Tuesday 25th August – Thursday 3rd September.

I was on the 12-4 for the first part of this trip and we saw a lot of ships every watch until Ceylon. I seem to have grown accustomed to the boredom of watches, or just keeping a lookout, because the hours haven't been dragging recently. On the 12-4 we do the weather, write up the slate, work an error and 0400 and 1600 D.R. This occupies about an hour if not rushed and time passes.

Thursday morning we tested the steering gear and I was on the poop wheel. Some difficulty was found in the air system and the rudder jammed hard to port twice. All afternoon the engineers worked on the mechanism and at 1600 we tested it again; this time was success. We sighted Ceylon Saturday afternoon at about 1400 and on Sunday John and I changed watches, which neither of us were very keen to do! However, this gave me a chance to get down to some 'bronzying' and office work. We began to have a lot of rain showers off Ceylon and Sunday night they obliterated Minicoy.

Monday, the winds began to freshen although the rain left us. Tuesday was very much cooler and we were pitching heavily at times. Wednesday morning at 0718 we sighted Socotra and altered course. The morning's watch was quiet but the lee of Socotra didn't live up to its name and until about 1100 we were still taking heavy seas occasionally. The evenings watch past uneventfully and we had stopped pitching. Thursday morning was fine with only two or three ships including the *"Menelaus"* which we picked up on radar going from Guardafui to Perim. We talked to her over the VHF and found that she was going to Alexandria for bunkers. We arrived at the Pilot at 2015 but had to wait until about 2100 before we could go in. We were all fast by 2200.

Aden.
Thursday 3rd September – Friday 4th September.
We had five cases to discharge from #1 for which we raised one Derrick and had a very large lighter alongside. These were finished by 2300 and then I had nothing to do. At midnight I called John and expecting to be on call for stand-by just crashed on the settee. Stand-by was at 0230 and we were away at 0342.

The first thing I knew was that it was 0700 and I hadn't been called for stand-by.

Aden to Suez.
Friday 4th September – Monday 7th September.
We were on the course for Perim before 0800 and by 0950 we were off Perim itself. There was a lot of traffic and by noon we were well into the Red Sea. At 1000 we were at Hells Gates and when I went on watch at 2000. The horizon was packed with ships. We had a rather unpleasant watch downwind of a tanker, which was emitting vast quantities of diesel fumes.

Saturday morning I turned to at 0800 on lifeboat stores and had then had them all out to be checked by 1100. During the afternoon the 3rd Mate and I checked and repacked them and at 1615 we had a boat and fire drill. The evenings watch was deadly quiet at first, but after we saw a couple of ships and one called us up.

Sunday we changed watches and I only did the 8-12 in the morning. We should have sighted St. John's Island at 1100, but we hadn't seen it by 1200. During the afternoon I did some more sunbathing and hung out my gear to air. We passed Daedalus reef during the afternoon and at midnight we were abeam of the Brothers. The weather has been most pleasant and Monday mornings watch was very cool. We passed about eleven ships and at 0345 picked up Shadwan Island on the radar. We altered onto 316 degrees at about 0420. We had another two alter courses before noon and during the 12-4 we had one at 1520. We slowed down for anchoring at 1612 and we were brought up at 1636.

Suez Canal Transit.
Port Said.
Monday 7th September – Wednesday 9th September.
We shifted ship at 1900 to an anchorage past Newport Rock. We were brought up at 2012. We were on anchor watches with the Mates and my job included making sure the three seaman

on deck patrol were patrolling. We weighed anchor at 0930 and entered the canal at 1030. By noon we weren't far from the Bitter Lakes and at 1244 we entered the Little Bitter Lake. At 1412 we anchored and waited for the two ships astern of us to overtake. At 1454, we were underway again. We reached Lake Timsah at 1640 and changed Pilots. We passed the cut at 1800 and we were in Port Said by 2200.

We had some cargo to discharge which was finished in less than an hour and at midnight when I went on the bridge the gear had been tested. The Pilot was aboard at 0020 and then began a frustrating wait for four tankers and a small Japanese fisherman. We were clear of the wharf at 0112 and full speed away was at 0200. When we retarded the clocks 60 minutes at 0245 we were on the alter course position off Damietta. The weather is much more pleasant now the temperature being in the upper 70s.

Port Said – Liverpool.
Wednesday 9th September – Thursday 17th September.
The afternoon watch was very quiet and really quite boring. After cleaning the brass on the wing repeater I had nothing to do until my afternoon sight.

Thursday morning was quite cool and passed on uneventfully. During the afternoon we sighted several ships, all either too far north or south of us to be of any interest. Friday was again cool and by noon we were on bearings with Malta. At 1805 we passed the "*Antilochus*" outward bound.

Saturday morning we were on bearings with Cape Bon at midnight and by 0400 we had passed Ile Cani and Ras Angela was just aft of the beam. We altered course about 0600 and at 0900 the "*Glenogle*" went leaping past. During the afternoon we were on radar bearings and as usual I just kept lookout, something which really got me down outward bound, but now I am used to it. This voyage has been a great disappointment to me because I was given the impression that we were to have responsibility, instead, I'm reduced to a lookout in broad daylight with no satisfaction at all. Weaker wills than mine could easily be broken by such treatment.

Sunday morning we were once again quite busy with ships and during the afternoon we took a noon sight at 1227. We changed watches and I went on the 8-12 during the evening. The visibility was not too good at first and eventually was down to three miles. We were on radar bearings and by midnight the visibility was up to 10 miles and we were 28 miles off Europa Point.

We were abeam at 0147 and when I went on watch Monday morning we had past Trafalgar. We altered off St. Vincent and at 1400 and by this time the wind had freshened. During the evening we had a great deal of traffic and we altered onto 000 degrees at 2136.

Tuesday morning our bearings weren't too good and by noon we had only just sighted Finisterre on the radar. We entered the Bay of Biscay at about 1530. At about 1300 we started rolling heavily and this was due to a south-westerly swell. Wednesday morning we left the Bay and by noon we were halfway across the channel. We went on to double watches at 1600 and John and I worked dog watches. We sighted Bishops Rock at 1730 and at 2000 we were well into the Bristol Channel. We hadn't sighted the Stack by midnight.

At 0400 we were on bearings which at 0500 we spotted the loom of the Stack Lighthouse. At 0730 we reduced to arrive at the Pilot on time and at 0800 the stack was abeam. We anchored at 1230 until 1630. We hove up and then anchored again proceeding in then at 1730. We were in the locks at 1930 and all fast by 2030. John and I went ashore after seeing the customs and we left the ship 1000 Friday 18th.

What We Learnt...

The log entries on this voyage, his eighth reported in the log, was much more detailed on the navigation between ports and what did or did not occur on the watches. Having finally bought some goods (Binoculars) rather than just 'shopping' it was somewhat amusing to read that there was not much to see with them between Aden and Penang.

It was always assumed that multiple cargos were being transported across the globe in these ships, tar, oil, tea for example are obvious. Cars and pineapples not so much – but I guess that shows more of my ignorance that anything else.

While there was a lot more seamanship and navigation mentioned in the log, there was still the painting and decorating to be taken care of and of course killing beetles and showing women in port around the ship – not sure that this would be allowed in this modern era.

"This voyage has been a great disappointment to me because I was given the impression that we were to have responsibility, instead, I'm reduced to a lookout in broad daylight with no satisfaction at all. Weaker wills than mine could easily be broken by such treatment."

While the above statement showed the frustration of P. J. Wood being on watch, he did manage to sight and more importantly avoid numerous Japanese fishing boats, Chinese Junks, Tankers and a self-propelled oil rig even with some super refraction to cope with. With the added bonus of some shooting stars.

This just shows that even if you personally may find the task beneath you or not understand the importance of it, you ultimately helped in your own small way to get the ship from Birkenhead to Liverpool via the Far East for 108 days without major incident.

S.S. HECTOR

October 1964
Voy. 38

Master: S. S. Howie
Mate: L. Henshall
2nd Mate: A. D. Denham
X/2nd Mate: J. M. Hughes
3rd Mate: M. E. G. Leale

<u>Cadet Officers</u>
P. J. Wood
C. O. Clowes

<u>Midshipman</u>
B. R. Situmeang

<u>Cadet Officers (E)</u>
L. J. McDonald
G. R. Jones

"Studies will be set for you during each voyage and you will be expected to complete these and return them, together with a report to the Managers, when your vessel returns to this country. Your report will inform the Managers of the way in which your time was spent at sea and at port."

- *Midshipman Appointment Letter from Alfred Holt & Co. circa 1960*

Voyage of S.S. Hector - Map

Voyage Statistics

Saturday 17th October 1964 - Liverpool - Joined Ship

Saturday 31st October 1964 - Port Said

Suez Canal Transit

Thursday 5th November 1964 - Aden

Tuesday 17th November 1964 - Freemantle

Sunday 22nd November 1964 - Adelaide

Thursday 26th November 1964 - Melbourne

Sunday 13th December 1964 - Sydney

Sunday 20th December 1964 - Brisbane

1st of January 1965 - Melbourne

Thursday 14th January 1965 - Adelaide

Monday 18th January 1965 - Albany

Sunday 31st January 1965 - Aden

Wednesday 3rd February 1965 - Suez

Suez Canal Transit

Thursday 4th of February 1965 - Port Said

Friday 12th February 1965 – Liverpool

Total number of Ports visited: 15
Total Voyage time: 118 days
Total Voyage Distance*: 25,040 Nautical miles

* All distances are estimated using Reed's New Maritime Distance Tables (1965) [Acquired from Fenton Steamship Co.

Chartering and S&P department] and by going "old school" with Lloyds Atlas of World Shipping Ports (30th Edition). Ports, wharfs, jetties and buoys have all changed dramatically over the last 62 years so that calculating accurate distances is nearly impossible to determine, so we used our best judgement.

Liverpool.

Saturday 17th October 1964 – Saturday 24th October 1964.

I left the hostel for the "*Hector*[55]" at 1030 with some personal effects belonging to Lyne. I was on board and unpacked by 1200. I went ashore during the afternoon and slept aboard the "*Jason*[56]" that night. Sunday morning, I returned aboard at 0900 and stood by as cargo was being worked. Monday I waited for 'specials' until 1700 and then tallied them until 1900. I went ashore during the evening and was aboard at midnight.

At 0800 I started the specials again and by 0900 all the Fremantle had finished. These were then blocked off with general and the Adelaide 'specials' began at 1030. I went ashore during the evening to the film "Goldfinger" and saw it for a second time. Afterwards I collected my gear from Lime Street left luggage and returned to the ship. All special cargo was finished by lunchtime when Chris joined.

Thursday morning we signed on and had our pre-voyage interviews and medical. At lunchtime we met John Martin quite by accident and had a good 'chin wag'.

Friday morning we took some trunks down to the luggage room but otherwise nothing special cropped up. We spent Saturday morning having fire and boat drills and doing a stowaway search. Stand-by went at 1300 and we let go at 1315. We went straight through the locks and the gangway stand-by was all over by 1400.

Liverpool – Port Said.

Saturday 24th October – Saturday 31st October.

We spent some time taking D.F. bearings of Bar Lightvessel and then proceeded to Holyhead I was on the 4-8 and then we rounded the Skerries at 1725. The Pilot was away at 1815 and we were full away at 1824. We sighted Bishops Rock Lighthouse beam at 0615 and by 0800 we were well into the channel.

Sunday morning our watches were changed and I went on to the 12-4 and Chris onto the 8-12 so Mr. Hughes our esteemed 2nd Mate could do the 4-8 and receive sea time for the voyage We were out of the bay by 2200 Sunday. Monday morning we had to spend a lot of time soogying the arcus, but otherwise all was quiet. Monday afternoon we had quite a lot of traffic and I took an error and did the humidity machine.

Tuesday morning at midnight we were approaching St. Vincent and at 0222 we altered off 111 degrees. At 1145 we alter off Cape Tarifa and at 1226 we were abeam of Europa point. Wednesday noon we were north of Algiers and Thursday morning at 0220 we altered off Galite Island. At 0900 we were abeam of Pantelleria and we had picked up Malta by 1515. From then on all was quiet and Friday we had a boat and fire drill at 1615. Saturday evening we arrived at Port Said and when I went on watch at midnight the northbound convoy was still coming out.

Port Said.
Canal Transit.
Sunday 1st November – Monday 2nd November.
All through the 12-4 we awaited instructions, but even at 0400 the northbound convoy was still coming out. I turned in optimistically and was called to go on the wheel at 0530. We passed the *"Pyrrhus"* discharging cargo homeward bound and were all fast by 0700. I then found a boat and read the draft, unfortunately only giving one draft chit out, to the Mate. I then turned in pessimistically and was called at 1100 for lunch. We entered the cut at 1424 and we were all fast by 1515. We left the cut at 2045 and when I went on watch we were in The Great Bitter Lakes. At 0300 we changed Pilots at Suez and at 0320 that Pilot was away, at 0330 we steadied on 184 degrees and F.S.A. was rung.

Suez – Aden.
Monday 2nd November – Thursday 5th November.
It is my turn to clean the bathroom this week, so I was hoping for an early start, unfortunately Chris didn't call me and I didn't wake up until 0900. I then had to collect my clean linen, clean

the bathroom, put my settee covers on and then stream the log. The morning passed quickly. During the afternoon we passed the "*Canberra*[57]" northbound, an altered course off Shaker Island at 1240. We were off bearings by 1330 and we picked up the Brothers at 1615. By midnight we had passed Daedalus Reef. The weather is quite warm for the time of year, though not unpleasant. The two dogs, Mitch and Sooty, are feeling a little under the weather though.

Wednesday we were on bearings during the afternoon and picked up Hells Gates at 1500. We passed through them at about 1700. By midnight we were on our penultimate course for Aden and at 0410 the Pilot was on board. I went on the wheel and Chris was called for the movement book. We were all fast by 0515. When I read the draft.

Aden.
November 5th.
I turned in almost immediately and got up at smoko when I vainly attempted to buy a pair of binoculars for four pounds. By 1115 the oil had finished and I got another draft. Stand-by went at 1145.

Aden – Fremantle.
Thursday November 5th – Tuesday 17th November.
After the gangway had been heaved up and lashed and the Pilot ladder rigged, I relieved Chris on the bridge. The Pilot left at about 1210. And we were clear of the harbour by 1220. F.S.A. was at 1224 and we were steadied on 096 degrees for Guardafui at 1300. The weather was very pleasant and there were no ships. Friday morning there was no traffic and the watch went peacefully. By 0900 when I went on the bridge for a sight we were on bearings with Guardafui. We were still just on bearings at noon and by 1400 the land had gone, the last until Australia.

Saturday mornings watch was very quiet as the next twelve or so night watches should be. We were steering 121 degrees and all was well. The weather became better as we approached the equator, though there was quite a good south-westerly swell. We crossed the line at 1030 Monday morning, but the water in the basin still goes down the same way. We had some rain showers during the afternoon, the first precipitation we've had since the Channel, otherwise that day was quiet.

Tuesday mornings watch was as usual and when I woke up at 0815 I took a sight; the days have settled into fairly good routine, after the morning sight I clean my room and do a couple of odd jobs before smoko, after which I get down to some bronzying and rule learning. After 1600, Chris and I usually have a game of deck tennis and before chow have a drink and a chat. During the evening I either have a game of cards, read, write or turn in early.

Wednesday mornings watch was a long one, four hours, as there was no clock flog. We had frequent rain showers and really it was quite a dismal watch. At 0800 the weather was fine and after taking a sight I did some revision for my first maths exam, which I shall be taking this afternoon. The exam was quite easy, although I made plenty of bloomers and I was not allowed to use the full edition of Nories i.e., with the explanations. The evening was spent arguing as to whether the full edition meant just the tables or the tables and the explanations.

Thursday mornings watch was helped by having a post-mortem on the maths paper and other than a little rain all was quiet. After the usual morning sight I did some more study and 1130 came round all too quickly. During the afternoons watch I did the first of the principles papers and I was quite happy with it.

Friday the 13th. It was much cooler during the whole of the day and especially during the morning. I had a third exam during the afternoon and didn't do at all that well with it. The watch passes much quicker though and I enjoy the exams. We had a boat drill at 1615 and a quick-fire drill.

Saturday was another fine day and during the afternoon watch I did my last exam of paper one. Sunday we changed back into 'Blues' and felt quite warm during the day, but quite cool after dark. Monday evening we picked up Rottnest Light at about 2200 and when I went on the bridge at midnight we were on a slow speed before anchoring. We anchored at 0036 and we were brought up at 0054. After writing up the slate the 2nd Mate let me turn in.

Fremantle.
Tuesday 17th November – Thursday 19th November.

I did the morning and tallied 'specials' from the poop cargo space. After lunch John, Barry and I went into Perth where we did some sightseeing and shopping. We returned aboard at 1800 and I did the evening. After cargo had finished at 2130, we shifted ship down to shed 'D' to make room for two passenger ships.

Wednesday morning I went aboard the "*Orcades*[58]" to see some friends only to find out they had already vacated their cabin and left. I then went around Fremantle and did some shopping. During the afternoon Chris and Geoff went into Perth and I spent the afternoon on deck. During the evening neither of us was required, so we went to a dance at the Flying Angel. The half dozen girls had no shortage of partners.

Thursday morning #1, #3, #5 and #7 finished before lunch and there were only fifteen drums to come out of the fore cabin. After lunch stand-by went at 1515 and I was on the gangway. F.S.A. was at 1606. The weather since our arrival had been cold at night, hot and cloudy during the day.

Fremantle – Adelaide.
Thursday 19th November – Sunday 22nd November.

We had changed watches and I am now on the 4-8. We left Fremantle north of Rottness Island and we set course 202 degrees at 1709. At 1715. The Mate went down, leaving me alone, which did a great deal for my spirits. By 2000 we were halfway towards the next alter course. Friday morning at 0400 we were steering 121 degrees and at 0639 we altered onto 097 degrees. By 0800 Chatham Island was abaft the beam. We entered the Great Australian Bight just after noon. At 1600 we had boat drill and afterwards I started to work out stars. This stretched my memory back a long time, but I had them all fixed by star time at 1945.

Saturday at 0400 I started to work out my stars immediately as star time was at 0500. I am attempting to get good results from air navigation tables, but so far I have not succeeded. After stars, the Mate went down again and the watch passed quickly as I did the humidity machine and worked out my morning sight. We had an engine room fire drill at 0930. Weather has been good for us, a force 7 wind astern but we're rolling easily. The evenings watch went quickly again and I made a classic mistake in my stars, using the wrong GMT.

Sunday morning I managed to reasonable answer in my stars, and this gave me a little encouragement. Sunday afternoon we picked up Kangaroo Island and by 1600 we were well into Investigator Strait. We altered course at 1835 and we anchored at 2030 off Port Adelaide Outer Harbour.

Adelaide.
Sunday 22nd November – Tuesday 24th November.

We were brought up by 2045 and we had to wait until 0540

Monday for the Pilot. We commenced to weigh anchor 0630 and followed the Port Nicholson into the outer harbour. One was needed whilst cargo was working, so Chris and Barry did that between them and I did the night. During the afternoon Chris and I went into the city of Adelaide. We returned aboard for chow. During the night all was quiet. We were supposed to sail about 1600, but this was put back to 1900 and we eventually let go at 2000. I was on the bridge and stayed up until we steadied on 201 degrees.

Adelaide – Melbourne.
Tuesday 24th November – Thursday 26th November.

We passed through Backstairs passage at 2300 and 0515 we picked up Cape Jaffa on the radar. By 0800 we were abeam of Rivoli Bay. At 1600 we were about 38 miles from Cape Otway alter course. However, we went round the corner in the in three easy stages and I was kept busy transferring charts, putting her down etc. At 2000 we were just on bearings with Split Point. I was to be up for the Pilot at about 2200 and stayed up until after he was aboard. We anchored off Port Melbourne at 0030 Thursday with the idea of going inside Friday.

Melbourne.
Thursday 26th of November – Friday 11th December.

I went on anchor watch at 0400 and there were seven ships as well as us anchored. By 0800 this number was down to three. During the day we started working 4 on, 12 off. The 2nd Mate, 3rd Mate, Chris and myself each doing a watch in turn. I did the evening 4-8 and the wind had strengthened to about force 6. We paid out more cable at 1720, but otherwise there wasn't much doing. After we had just paid out the cable, the breakwater signal station called us up and had a message for us from the agent to pick up the TV sets on Friday at 1500. During the evening Chris and I had a couple of games of cards. On Friday I did the 8-12 during the morning. Most of my time was spent learning Rule 9.

Saturday morning the wind had died down and I was able to

do some study. At 0900 I started my second maths exam, by 1115 I had finished all I could do. We changed watches and I did the 12-4 during the afternoon. It was a beautiful afternoon and there were many yachts out during the afternoon.

Sunday morning I did the 4-8 and the weather was very pleasant, though cold. After breakfast I did some study and sunbathing. I did the 8-12 during the evening and it was quite cool by 2300.

Monday I was called at 0540 to wait until stand-by, this eventually went at 0640 and I went on the bridge for the wheel. By 0830 we had just entered the River Yarra and I went down to breakfast then, after which I stood by the gangway. We were all fast by 0940 and as we didn't have any gangs Chris and I had the rest of the day off until the evening.

Tuesday we had seven gangs, so I did the morning we worked #1, #3, #4, #5 and #6. I went ashore during the afternoon and did some shopping. During the evening Chris and I went to the pictures and saw "The Thrill of it all".

Wednesday we changed to working day about and I did the day. During the morning I tallied specials from #1 strong room. During the afternoon work continued with special attention to the fridge lockers in #3 and #4. During the evening, Chris and I saw a variety show at the Mission which was quite enjoyable.

Thursday was my day off and I was able to catch up on some dhobi and letter writing. Friday cargo continued smoothly though the weather turned cooler. The "*Helenus*[59]" came in and we arranged to meet Pete Wallace and Goodlan on Saturday afternoon.

Saturday the weather turned showery and we weren't able to go swimming as we had hoped. Instead we watched the television and had a very quiet afternoon. We went to a party during the evening which lasted until Sunday 5 AM. I was on Sunday rather unfortunately there were seven gangs so I did the morning and then the 3rd Mate did the afternoon.

Monday, the weather was again much worse but I was able to do some more letter writing. Monday evening Chris and I again went to the pictures.

Tuesday we started #7 and I tallied some specials from the poop locker. That evening we had to start heating a tank of oil which is stowed on the port side of the aft well deck. The idea was to heat the oil until the top half an inch was 115 degrees and then turn off, stir, wait half an hour and then start again. No water could contaminate the oil so as heavy rain started lashing down about 1800, the idea was abandoned until the next day.

We went onto 6 on, 12 off as the oil would be a little tedious. I did the 12-6 during the afternoon as we had been invited out to dinner by some friends of the Old Man's. Barry did the evening. We had a most enjoyable evening and returned to the ship about 2330.

Thursday we continued with the oil and did the 12-6. During the afternoon Chris and I went to shore and did some shopping. Friday we sailed at last at 1700. After being on stand-by for an hour, I was on the bridge. The 3rd Mate went down when I was relieved and when we were clear of the river, the Old Man left me up with the Pilot.

Melbourne – Sydney.
Friday 11th December – Sunday 13th December.

We entered the channel to Port Philip Heads at 1934. At 2000 we rigged the pilot ladder and boat rope. The Pilot left at 2030 and I then turned in. By 0400 we were on the departure position with Chaffy Island. The weather has really deteriorated now and we are now rolling quite heavily. At 0600 we sighted the *"Helenus"* ahead, we were overtaking her and at about 1000 she altered 90 degrees to starboard. We were in the bad weather until we rounded the headland and the swell then died down. During the evening 4-8 we had good visibility and bearings were plentiful. At about 0020 we picked up the Pilot and at 0215 I was called for gangway stand-by. We were all Fast at 0300.

Sydney.
Sunday 13th December – Saturday 19th December.

We stayed on sea watches until 0800 and then started the heating of the oil. Barry and I went ashore during the afternoon and had a look around the town the *"Helenus"* came in at about 1400, just twelve hours astern of us but we weren't on the bridge to see it. We looked around Circular Quay, went up the lookout tower of the bridge and ended up aboard the *"Helenus"* in Walsh Bay. We returned to Wooloomooloo at about 1700.

I had been on the oil during the morning and started again at midnight. Next day Barry and Chris started sixes on the oil whilst I did the twilights for the 2nd Mate, the 3rd Mate being laid up. Chris and I went to Manly and visited Marineland where we saw the fish being fed by hand. After visiting the small and interesting Shark Aquarium, we returned to the ship. Tuesday afternoon we met Pete Wallace and went to Taronga Park Zoo and spent a very interesting afternoon looking around. Chris and I were working again during the evening.

Wednesday, Geoff and I went to Bondi Beach at 10 o'clock. It was wonderful day and we had a very interesting time. At 1430 Chris turned up with Pete and Rick from the *"Helenus"* we then hired some rubber floats and tried surfing. We returned to the ship that chow time. I was on oil during the evening.

Thursday morning I was on oil again and the temperature is more now than when we started but even so, we aren't too enthusiastic about the job anymore. During the afternoon I stayed aboard and that evening Chris and I went to a Christmas party at the Red Ensign Club.

Friday morning we heard that the oil would not be discharged until Melbourne homeward bound since the lorry drivers have gone on strike. Our job then was to remove the coils and screw down the tank.

Saturday morning I brine sealed the #3 lower hold and #4 U.T.D. centre lockers. We tested gear at 1615 and I went on bridge stand-by. We had to wait for tugs and the *"Tjiwangi*[60]*"* to sail, so we didn't clear the wharf until 1715. The Pilot was away at 1749 and Full Speed Away was rung at 1754. We overtook the *"Tjiwangi"* at 1815.

Sydney – Brisbane.
Saturday 19th December – Sunday 20th December.
The voyage was very quiet and the weather improved. We entered Moreton Bay at 1730 and S.B.E. for picking up the Pilot was 1824. The Pilot was aboard at 1852 and we entered the buoyed channel at 1730. We anchored 2120 await the tide.

Brisbane.
Monday 21st December – Tuesday 29th December.
We tested gear to move in at 0430 and we had to wait until the *"Tjiwangi"* had passed before we proceeded. The anchor was away at 0524 and we were up to our berth at 0730. We had five gangs discharging and, as usual, one of us was on. I was on the night. Tuesday morning we moved up to Hamilton Wharf to load fridge cargo. We then move back to Mercantile on Christmas Eve. We were all fast by 1200 and then no work was to start until Monday. Chris and I went ashore to do some shopping and have a swim during the afternoon.

Christmas Day.
I was on the night and was not called until 1100 when after having a shower, I went down to the lounge. We were in there until lunchtime, which was about 2 PM. Lunch took quite a long time and wasn't very enjoyable as people kept moving around and making speeches. However lunch, or should I say, dinner was over about 3:30 PM when we all returned to our beds for respite. At 6:30 I surfaced to find no one else up so I roused John, Geoff, Chris, and Barry and we started again. The Queen's Speech was on at 7:15 which was watched by most when no one felt like much. The five of us then joined the sailors and the stewards in a sing song by #6 hatch. Again, I was on the night.

Boxing Day.
Today we are up early and we went riding, Horse riding, that is. The place was about two miles past Chemside tram terminal and was called Aspley Riding Ranch. Our nags were quite dependable

– If nothing else and we had a good ride for two hours or so during the afternoon. Chris and I went swimming to loosen up our muscles, some of which had only just we had only just discovered.

Sunday, the last day of the holiday saw us visiting the Lone Pine Koala Sanctuary, which is almost 12 miles from Brisbane by river. The place was small but novel and we had our photos taken holding a bear. They weren't as cuddly as they look, but just as docile. They sleep 18 hours a day and live entirely on eucalyptus leaves and doesn't even drink. That evening we turned in early.

Monday morning everyone had the post-holiday blues and work went quite quietly. We were still loading fridge cargo in #3 and #4 lower holds and we started general in #2, #5, #6 and #7. The weather was warm but not too hot with a little rain.

Tuesday I was off during the day and was able to do some shopping, but during the evening I turned in as we were to sail at midnight. At 2315 we tested gear and at midnight we were underway. When I went onto the bridge at 0400 we were approaching the estuary of the river and at 0430 the Pilot was away. Full Speed Away was 0436.

Brisbane to Melbourne.
30th of December 1964 to 1st of January 1965.

We then started out of Moreton Bay and at 0600 altered down the coast. There was quite a heavy south-easterly swell running and we rolled easily. Other than that, the weather was fine and clear. The evenings watch was busy as usual, taking bearings and doing the humidity machine. Thursday morning at 0400 we were just about level with Sydney and the "*Arcadia*[61]" was abeam bound for Sydney. We were still rolling but the swell had died down. At noon we were only just on bearings and we just managed it for stars as well.

Friday morning when we came on watch we had just altered onto the last course before Port Philip Heads. At 0730 we called Point Lowsdale on the VHF and at 0600 I had altered course of my own accord for the first time. That is for a ship. The

"*Ellinis*[62]", Chandris lines and I felt very chuffed to do it. We picked up the Pilot at 0920 and I was on the bridge for passing through the heads. At 1000 we started celebrating New Year in England and by noon we had done Dublin as well. We L.G. port anchor at 1154.

Melbourne.
Friday 1st January 1965 – Wednesday 13th January.

We were anchored until Tuesday and nothing much happened out of the ordinary. The most important job of the anchor watch was to keep the TV aerial pointing in the right direction. The weather was warm but not spectacular and some nights were quite cold. The wind was quite strong for a couple of days.

We berthed early morning on Tuesday 5th of January and at lunchtime we started on our cursed oil stirring. We started 6 on, 12 off on the job and this lasted until Saturday morning. Not much happened to us until then, and I was glad when the pump men from Mayne Nickless arrived. The tank contained thirty tons in two separate sections and pumping took about four hours from start to finish. When that was complete, Chris, Barry and I all turned to and cleared up the mess. We were then off until Monday except one on the nights, which was Barry. That evening we went to a party ashore and had a very enjoyable time, all that is except the fridge man who was arrested, and we arrived back aboard about 4 AM Sunday. After lunch Chris and I went for a swim at Mr and Mrs Gillons and met their daughter and her friend and this turned out to be one of the best afternoons I've had for ages.

Monday morning we turned to at 0600 to dress ship overall. Monday, 11th of January being the company's centenary. By the time we had finished it was almost eight, so we immediately hoisted them. We then found out the Spanish ensign was the second flag of the aft hoist. Luckily, I was able to go up the mast and cut it off before any diplomatic ties were severed. That evening there was a ship's party and I showed the guests, including Mr and Mrs Gillon, up the up to the lounge.

Tuesday I was on until just after lunch when the Mate said I could knock off as the Gillons had asked us to their house for the afternoon. We arrived to find them out, so we waited and eventually they arrived about four o'clock. I stayed to dinner, though Chris went after having just a steak and I was given a lift back to the ship by Robert Denham. After showing him around the ship and having a beer he left. We sailed Wednesday evening and I was on the bridge for stand-by. We were clear of the river at 1900 and the Pilot was away at 2150. Port Philip Heads is one of the only places I dislike doing the pilot gear and it was my job every time.

Melbourne – Adelaide.
Wednesday 13th January – Thursday 14th January.
Full Speed Away was at 2200 and 0400 Thursday we were on bearings. The day was fine after the rotten weather of the last two days in Melbourne. Thursday evening we picked up and passed through Backstairs Passage and we altered course at 1630 and anchored off the Fairway Buoy at 2200.

Adelaide.
Thursday 14th January – Saturday 16th January.
At 0530 Friday we tested the gear and the Pilot was aboard at 0600. We commenced to weigh anchor and then for stand-by I was on the wheel and we ran lines at the outer harbour at 0657. We were all fast at 0700, but cargo did not begin until 0830. I was on during the morning and during the afternoon we went to Semaphore Beach which was not much good compared with Bondi. When we returned aboard, we found that Peter McBride had phoned inviting us sailing. Chris, myself and the 1st Engineer went and we had an enjoyable sail despite the lack of wind. We returned to the moorings about eleven and after coffee and biscuits we were given a lift back to the ship. Chris was on midnight and I was on at 0600. The gangs knocked off at 0620 with time for washing etc. and we finished work at 1130. We then tested gear and sailed immediately looking like a Hong

Kong Sampan with all the derricks flying.

Adelaide – Albany.
Saturday 16th January – Monday 18th January.
The Pilot was away at 1232 and by 1600 we were just about out of Investigator Strait north of Kangaroo Island. Sunday morning the swell was much worse and at 1600 we were rolling very heavily, so we reduced to 15 1/2 knots. We stayed reduced until 0615 Monday morning. We increased then and made the landfall at 1700 that evening. S.B.E. was 2142 and we were anchored off Albany at 2227.

Albany.
Tuesday 19th January.
The Pilot was due at 0500, so we tested gear at 0430. The Pilot arrived shortly before five and hove up immediately. I was on the wheel for stand-by and we were all fast with two anchors for'd and lines to the buoy aft at 0648. We started pumping at 0750 and had all deep tank in #5 to fill. We were not required but during the afternoon Chris went out with the 2nd Mate in a boat to sound round off the starboard quarter. Pumping finished at 1830 and the gear was tested at 1842. There was no Pilot for leaving and S.B.E. was at 1928. Both anchors were away at 1950.

Albany – Aden.
Tuesday 19th January – Sunday 31st January.
F.S.A. was at 2000 and I was on the wheel until we cleared the heads and then I wrote up the slate. There was quite a big swell running, but when we set course we were only rolling easily. Wednesday morning we were on bearings until 0600 and although we could see the land until about 0700, that was our departure position. The rest of the trip was mainly without incident. The weather improved as we travelled further north until a couple of days south of the equator when we started having frequent rain showers. We saw only one ship after leaving Albany until Guardafui and that was the *"English Star*[63]*"* which we passed on the first day.

I was still on the 4 to 8 and was kept busy on watch working all stars, taking sights and doing the humidity machine. On Monday the 26th we reduced for half an hour to test the emergency steering gear. Chris was on the poop, Barry in the steering flat and I was on the bridge. We had an emergency lifeboat drill on Tuesday the 27th, which again only took half an hour. I went in the boat and Chris went on the bridge. The drill was all over by 0945. We crossed the equator at 0800 Thursday morning and from then on the weather improved. We made the landfall with Ras Kalan at 0500 on Saturday the 30th and we altered course off Guardafui at 1030. The evenings watch passed quickly with what was to us, a lot of traffic. We made the landfall with Aden at 0400 Sunday morning and we had the Pilot on board 0650. We were all fast by 0745.

Aden.
Sunday, 31st of January.
We had very little cargo work. One car to load in #6 and 46 drums to discharge from #1. Chris, Barry and I went ashore at 0900 on the agents launch and did quite a lot of shopping. I bought an electric flash gun and electric toy and we returned to the ship at midday. We sailed at 1315 and I was on gangway stand-by.

Aden – Suez.
Sunday 31st January – Wednesday 3rd February.
I went on to the 8-12 as Mr. Hughes had finished his work and was to do the 4-8. At 2000 we were abeam of Perim Island and at 2005 we altered course. The watch was very busy with shipping and there was also a clock flog.

Monday morning was quite quiet and during the evening we picked up Jabol Amais "Hell Gates". We reached Hells Gates at about 0130 Tuesday. At noon we were approaching St. Johns Island but we didn't see it until 1300. That evening we were just between the Brothers and Daedalus Reef and by midnight we had picked up Daedalus light. We altered in the Gulf of Suez and at 0600 and the 8-12 was quite busy for ships. At 1330 the Pilot was on board and we anchored at 1400.

Suez Canal Transit.
Wednesday 3rd February – Thursday 4th February.
After getting a draught, I had nothing to do until 1800 when I did the chow relief. At 2000 I went on the bridge but was fortunately not required. The next morning we hove up and moved into the canal at 0930. The Pilot amused us all by asking for, receiving and then putting on a hernia belt in the wheelhouse. The smile soon disappeared from my face when I had to adjust it. We entered the Little Bitter Lake at 1130 and were anchored for half an hour at 1330. We changed Pilots at 1530. The cut was passed about 1800 and by 2000 we were not far from Port Said. We weren't stopping thank goodness and we left the canal at 2050. We set course at 2130 and the swell was very bad.

Port Said – Dunkirk, redirected Liverpool.
Thursday 4th of February –
We didn't ring full away, but at midnight the revs were 96. The swell was very heavy. We altered onto 288 degrees at 2330. Friday morning the weather had improved but still wasn't favourable. The evening 8-12 saw a sudden drop in the barometer and by 0600 we were rolling moderately. At 0745 we took some dangerous rolls and we went on to half speed. We gradually moved out of the depression and at 1006 F.S.A. was rung. By middle of the afternoon we were not rolling at all. The evenings 8-12 was much colder and at midnight we ran into quite a lot of rain. We were on bearings with Malta until 0620 and we picked up Pantellaria at 0900. We altered course again at 1030 on 288 degrees and at noon we had picked up Cape Bon.

Cape Bon was abeam just after 1300. We picked up Cape de Gata that evening at 2300. The next day we were abeam of Europa Point at 0945. We altered course at 1005 and again at 1050. By noon we were approaching Cape Trafalgar and we passed the "*Eumaeus*[64]" at 1155. The evenings watch was very busy and we altered course off St. Vincent at 2040. We entered the Bay of Biscay at 0600 Wednesday and by 0800 the weather had worsened to force 7, but fortunately by noon had decreased.

The best news of the voyage came Tuesday afternoon when we were re-directed to Liverpool. We left the Bay about 0800 Thursday and at 0245 we sighted Bishops Rock Lighthouse. When I went on watch at 2000 we were expecting to pick up The Smalls which eventually appeared at 2015 and we altered onto 005 degrees. At 2130 we were abeam of south Bishop and altered onto 026 degrees.

The Pilot was aboard at 0315. When I was called we were anchored off the Bar Lightvessel. We were at anchor until 1500 when we weighed anchor. chow was at 1600, when I relieved Chris at 1630 we were abeam of New Brighton Pier.

We entered the lock at 1715 and we were all fast alongside S.W. Langton at 1800. After taking our own gear to the station we returned to the ship.

We left the ship Saturday morning.

13th February 1965

What We Learnt...

Arriving to sign-on the Hector in Liverpool and somehow managing to sleep on the Jason that first night, maybe the beds were more comfortable, who is to know. It may not sound like the best start to his first voyage to Australia but let's not knock poor geography of bedrooms on various ships in the Blue Funnel Line.

This log definitely showed how P. J. Wood had grown over the previous 3 years. There was a definite feel for a "Work Hard, Play Hard" attitude in the log, from the detailed navigational information to the ecological and groundbreaking information from the Koala Sanctuary.

"They weren't as cuddly as they looked, but just as docile"

The BBC didn't lose out when they ultimately went for David Attenborough to front their nature shows.

I'm all for being honest in your log and the midshipman appointment letter actually makes a point of saying that you should. But the partying until 5am and arrests were surprising.

Another birthday onboard but this time in the middle of the Indian Ocean and having a maths exam – Oh! The adventure and thrill of a life at sea – this log has really sold it to me...

They spent Christmas off Brisbane – not the urban jungle that it is now, but a rainforest and couple of pubs apparently. The Company's centenary was celebrated in Melbourne and other than a mix up with some flags seemed to go well eventually.

Finally, my father loves a good cruise, or to that matter an indifferent cruise as long as it has in his words "decent sea time". I can see why this is - the legs between Aden and Australia being 10 days out of sight of land and other ships. He enjoyed that time, apart from the maths tests...

AFTER THE HALFDECK

"Finally, never forget that a free and enthusiastic interest in your life's work is a source of great happiness. Have a pride therefore in your Service and in your Company and contribute your full share to the common good. The management most earnestly desire that you should find lasting happiness and satisfaction in your association with the Company.
Wishing you a most successful career."

- *Midshipman Appointment Letter from Alfred Holt & Co. circa 1960*

1 year 4 months pre-sea training at the London Nautical School.

The adventures didn't stop after the S.S Hector in February 1965, but the log did, the final voyage as an apprentice midshipman was a coastal voyage again on the S.S. Hector but was apparently of not much importance or interest to the Managers for signing off the logbook and ultimately signing off the apprenticeship.

The personal log was not carried on past the apprenticeship as Alfred Holt & Co. did not allow personal logs for their officers as there was a risk that it may have contradicted or been in some way different to the slate and official log. Should something occur, the last thing the company wanted was confusion or worse, contradiction, with the official log.

In 1968 P. J. Wood had gained his Mate's ticket and decided that he would become a student at Plymouth Polytechnic (now known as Plymouth University) as he incorrectly thought it would three years ashore as a student. In 1972, he completed the BSc. in Navigation and Transport and got married.

During this period, containerisation was coming in and Blue Funnel had so many qualified people that while he had achieved his Mate's Ticket he was only employed on board as 2nd Mate, promotions required essentially waiting for dead men's boots - this was the standard practice of the Company.

His last voyage was on the Priam (where he was also joined by his wife and my wonderful mother Cathy) and went round the globe for the final time and gave him the required sea time to study for his Masters Ticket which, after 6 months of study ashore at Plymouth Nautical School was presented to him on 8th October 1974. Just one day shy of being exactly 13 years after he signed his Apprentice's Indenture.

Certificate of Competency – Master (Foreign-Going)

P. J. Wood decided to leave the sea when he had the opportunity to join the chartering department of Ocean Transport and Trading Group in London called Ocean McGregor.

He was accepted on to the Baltic Exchange in 1974 and since then served as either an Owner's Broker, Charterers Agent, or Competitive Broker.

In 1975 he qualified as AICS with Institute of Chartered Shipbrokers and in 1976 he developed an interest in the professional education in the shipping business and became FICS examiner Economics of Sea Transport, member of the Education Committee of ICS and lectured part time at the City of London Polytechnic on Economics of Sea Transport.

Between 1976-1981 he worked as an owner's broker, charterers agent and competitive broker covering various deep sea dry cargo trades from 7,000 DWT up to 70,000 DWT.

In 1981 he joined the Fenton Steamship Company European General Agents for Hellenic Lines as Chartering Manager for the tramping fleet of Bulk Carriers and Tankers managed by Trade & Transport Inc., Piraeus.

In 1984 he was the founding Director of Trade & Transport (UK) Ltd created to carry on the tramping activities of Trade & Transport Group after the demise of Hellenic Lines. The fleet make up varied but generally was a mixture of bulk carriers and tankers, mainly trading on the spot market.

Retiring in 2013, or at least semi-retiring, Philip carried on as a member of the ICS board of examiners and lecturing.

Other positions held:
- 1976-1999: Served on the Education Committee of ICS
- 1989-1999: Chairman Education Committee (ICS)
- 1997-1999: Vice Chairman Institute of Chartered Shipbrokers
- 1999-2001: Chairman Institute of Chartered Shipbrokers
- 2002: Chairman Board of Examiners and Assessors (ICS)
- FONASBA member, Chartering & Documentary Committee
- 2004-2006: President Federation of National

Associations of Shipbrokers and Agents (FONASBA)
Author of the textbook - "Tanker Chartering", published by Witherby & Co. In cooperation with the Institute of Chartered Shipbrokers.

Philip was at sea with the Blue Funnel Line for 4,400 days or 12 years and 17 days and for the last couple of years he and I have been procrastinating on transcribing, editing and publishing this book. We feel that with seven grandchildren to entertain him and the dent we have put in the wine lakes of Europe that the time was spent well.

This has been a labour of love for me, I've always been proud of him and his achievements and any excuse to spend time with him is a good reason; what could be better than getting him to talk to me about his life at sea?

What we are going to do in the next couple of years as the book has now been completed I don't know, by I am going to guess it may involve some "shopping".

SHIPS SERVED & RANKS

T he following is a list of all the ships P. J. Wood served on between 1961 and 1973 and as a Midshipman, Cadet Officer and Officer.

GLENROY.	3.11.61 - 8.01.62	Midshipman
ULYSSES.	29.01.62 - 10.07.62	Midshipman
AJAX.	11.07.62 - 29.07.62	Midshipman
GLENEARN.	09.11.62 - 08.12.62	Midshipman
GLENGYLE.	09.12.62 - 22.12.62	Midshipman
GLENARTNEY.	02.01.63 - 17.01.63	Midshipman
GLENOGLE.	23.05.63 - 16.09.63	Midshipman
CLYTONEUS.	10.10.63 - 17.01.64	Midshipman

AUTOMEDAN.	01.06.64 - 17.09.64	Cadet Officer
HECTOR.	17.10.64 - 13.02.65	Cadet Officer
HECTOR.	22.02.65 - 11.03.65	Cadet Officer

+ + + + + + +

GLENARTNEY.	07.09.65 - 24.09.65	Extra 3rd Mate
DEMODOCUS.	29.10.65 - 11.11.65	Extra 3rd Mate
DENBIGHSHIRE.	03.12.65 - 01.03.66	Extra 3rd Mate
DENBIGHSHIRE.	01.04.66 - 22.07.66	Extra 3rd Mate
DENBIGHSHIRE.	23.07.66 - 28.07.66	Extra 3rd Mate
MYRMIDON.	09.09.66 - 21.09.66	Extra 3rd Mate
MYRMIDON.	30.09.66 - 31.12.66	Extra 3rd Mate
MYRMIDON.	09.01.67 - 02.02.67	3rd Mate
GLENOGLE.	23.05.67 - 16.06.67	Extra 3rd Mate
DENBIGHSHIRE.	12.07.67 - 25.07.67	3rd Mate
CALCHAS.	09.08.67 - 03.12.67	3rd Mate
BALTIC ARROW. (U B C)	22.07.68 - 20.09.68	3rd Mate
RADNORSHIRE.	04.07.69 - 27.07.69	Acting 2nd Mate
RADNORSHIRE.	27.07.69 - 05.11.69	2nd Mate
RADNORSHIRE.	30.11.69 - 05.03.70	2nd Mate
RADNORSHIRE.	01.04.70 - 05.07.70	2nd Mate
RADNORSHIRE.	06.07.70 - 07.08.70	2nd Mate
GLENALMOND.	07.08.70 - 26.08.70	2nd Mate

GLENALMOND.	08.08.72 - 05.09.72	2nd Mate
GLENALMOND.	18.09.72 - 18.12.72	2nd Mate
PATROCLUS.	16.01.73 - 02.04.73	2nd Mate
PATROCLUS.	03.04.73 - 31.05.73	2nd Mate
PRIAM.	19.07.73 - 20.11.73	2nd Mate

The term 'Extra 3rd Mate' is technically 4th Mate, however when signing on it is listed as Extra 3rd Mate. Blue Funnel had so many qualified people that while P. J. Wood had achieved his Mates ticket he was only employed on board as 2nd Mate - this was the standard practice of the company at the time.

FOOTNOTES – VESSEL REFERENCE

[1] Stratheden – Built in 1937 – DWT: 23,732 – Built for the P&O Line. She was sold in 1964 to John Latsis, Piraeus, and renamed Henrietta Latsis.

[2] Glenfinlas – Built in 1946 – DWT: 7,639 – Completed as Calchas for China Mutual Steam Navigation Company (Taken over by Alfred Holt & Co. in 1902) In 1957 she was chartered to Glen Line and renamed Glenfinlas, in 1962 reverted to Calchas and in 1973 scrapped after fire at Kelang, Malaysia.

[3] Menelaus – Built in 1957 – DWT: 8,538 - In 1972 transferred to Elder Dempster Line, renamed Mano, in 1977 renamed Oti and in 1978 sold to Greece and renamed Elstar.

[4] Orestes – Built in 1924 – DWT: 7,845 – Scrapped in 1963.

[5] Glenroy – Built in 1938 – DWT: 9,809 – Scrapped in 1966.

[6] Soudan – Built in 1947 – DWT: 9,080 – Part of the P&O fleet, Scrapped in 1970.

[7] Perseus – Built in 1950 – DWT: 10,109 – Scrapped in 1973.

[8] Ascanius – Built in 1950 – DWT: 7,692 – In 1972 she was transferred to Elder Dempster Line and renamed Akosombo, in 1973 she reverted to Ascanius and in 1976 sold to Saudi-Europe Line where she was renamed Mastura.

[9] Ulysses – Built in 1949 – DWT: 8,976 – In 1971 sold to Cyprus and renamed Aegis Saga

[10] Battleship Texas (BB-35) – Launched in 1912 and decommissioned in 1948. The Battleship Texas was the first U.S. permanent battleship Museum.

[11] Agapenor – Built in 1947 – DWT: 7,664 – In 1967 she had to be abandoned to insurers after becoming trapped by closure of Suez Canal. In 1975 she became Panamanian registered and renamed Nikos.

[12] Oranje – Built in 1938 – DWT: 20,565 – Owned by Nederland Line, laid up and used as a hospital ship during the war, she was sold to Lauro Line, Italy in 1964, she was renamed Angelina Lauro.

[13] Ajax – Built in 1958 – DWT: 7,969 – In 1972 renamed Deucalion and in 1973 sold to Macao renamed Kailock.

[14] Antilochus – Built in 1949 – DWT: 7,635 – In 1977 she was sold to Gulf (Shipowners) Ltd, London and renamed Gulf Orient.

[15] Tantalus – Built in 1945 – DWT: 7,674 – Originally known as Polyphemus an ex- Macmurray Victory ship, in 1946 it was purchased from US Maritime Commission and renamed, operated by NSOM (Dutch), in 1960 transferred to Blue Funnel and renamed Tantalus, in 1969 sold to Greece renamed Pelops and scrapped.

[16] Bendoran – Built in 1956 – DWT: 10,142 – Completed for Ben Line Steamers Ltd. - Wm. Thomson & Co., Leith. In 1977 she was scrapped.

[17] Benavon – Built in 1949 – DWT: 7,845 – In 1970 sold to Panama and renamed Liziana.

[18] Bengloe – Built in 1961 – DWT: 11,282- Scrapped in 1978.

[19] Polydorus – Built in 1945 – DWT: 7,671 – ex- Salina Victory, in 1946 purchased from US Maritime Commission, renamed Polydorus, operated by NSOM (Dutch), 1960 transferred to Blue Funnel, renamed Talthybius during the 1960's, in 1971 she was scrapped.

[20] Elbe I Lightvessel (Lightship ELBE 1) – Launched in 1943, it did not go into service until 1948. While in operation it was considered the largest lightship in the world. Operations were stopped in 1988 and it is now a Maritime Museum located in Cuxhaven, Germany.

[21] Fleetbank – Built in 1953 – DWT: 5,690 – In 1970 she was sold to Lalis & Boudros, Greece and renamed Lady Ute.

[22] Tongue lightship – Tongue Sands [51°30'39"N 1°23'5"E]. Stationed in the North Sea, 8 miles north of Margate.

[23] Sunk Lightvessel – Sunk Sands [51°49'35"N 1°30'40"E]. Stationed in the Thames Estuary since 1802. It was replaced in 2007 by Sunk Centre as part of a new Traffic Separation Scheme.

[24] ELBE 3 Lightvessel – Built in 1888 as the Weser lightship. Since 1979 it now moored at the Övelgoenne museum harbour in Hamburg-Neumühlen

[25] S. Goodwin Lt. Ship – Goodwin Sands [51°13'18"N 1°36'21"E]. LV69 was sunk on station by a mine in October 1940. The replacement, LV90, sank on 27 November 1954 when cables to her two sea anchors broke in a hurricane-force storm. With the loss of seven souls. The next replacement ship was decommissioned on 26 July 2006.

[26] Royal Sovereign Lt. ship – Royal Sovereign shoals [50°43′24″N 0°26′08″E]. A sandbank 6.8 miles offshore of Eastbourne. The lightvessel was replaced with Royal Sovereign lighthouse 1971.

[27] Ixion – Built in 1951 – DWT: 10,125 – Scrapped in 1972.

[28] Autolycus – Built in 1949 – DWT: 7,635 – In 1976 she was sold to Gulf (Shipowners) Ltd based in London and renamed Gulf Trader.

[29] Flintshire – Built in 1962 – DWT: 11,926 – In 1978 sold to Liberia and renamed Orient Express.

[30] Stentor – Built in 1946 – DWT: 10,203 – In 1958 transferred to Glen Line and renamed Glenshiel. In 1963 she reverted to Stentor and in 1975 was scrapped.

[31] Despite our best efforts, unfortunately, we were unable to find the history of this vessel in the correct time period or at least any information that was available to research online.

[32] HMS Lion – Commissioned in 1960 – DWT: 12,080 – Having been rushed into service with some shortcuts in the engineering department, due to political pressure to get her to sea, but she was not fully operational until 1961. She reached the Far East in early 1963. She was present at the Malaya independence celebrations in 1963 and the Maltese independence celebrations in 1964 before being decommissioned in 1972.

[33] Laomedon – Built in 1953 – DWT: 7684 – In 1977 she was sold to Panama and renamed Aspasia.

[34] Despite our best efforts, unfortunately, we were unable to find the history of this vessel in the correct time period or at least any information that was available to research online.

[35] Himalaya – Launched in 1948 – DWT: 9,659 – S.S. Himalaya was P&O and operated mainly between United Kingdom and Australia. She was withdrawn from service in 1974 and scrapped the next year.

[36] HMS Albion – Commissioned in 1954 – DWT: 24,000 – Originally joining the Mediterranean fleet, she was part of the Suez crisis. In 1961 conversion begun to a commando carrier and she recommissioned in 1962 before joining the Far East Fleet. She had the nickname of "The Old Grey Ghost of the Borneo Coast" – She was scrapped in 1973.

[37] Pyrrhus – Built in 1949 – DWT: 10,093 – Scrapped in 1972.

[38] Cathay – Built in 1957 – DWT: 13,351 – In 1961 P&O purchased from CMB, Antwerp and renamed Cathay, in 1976 she was sold to China and renamed Kenghsin.

[39] Menestheus – Built in 1958 – DWT: 8,510 – In 1977 she was transferred to Elder Dempster Line and renamed Onitsha. In 1978 she

was sold to Cyprus and renamed Elisland.

[40] Glenogle – Built in 1962 – DWT: 11,918 – In 1978 she was sold to Hong Kong and renamed Harvest.

[41] Doctor Lykes – Built 1945 – DWT: 7,854 - Standard ship type C3-S-BH1 built for United States Maritime Commission, she was scrapped in 1973.

[42] Anchises – Built in 1946 – DWT: 7,642 – In 1973 she was renamed Alcinous and was scrapped in 1975.

[43] Clytoneus – Built in 1948 – DWT: 7,620 – Scrapped in 1972.

[44] Oronsay – Built in 1951 – DWT: 28,136 – Originally built for the Orient Line, in 1962 she was transferred to P&O Line and in 1975 she was scrapped.

[45] Bar Lightvessel – Mersey Bar [53°32'1"N 3°20'59"W] From 1960 to 1972 the vessel was stationed on Bar Station, Liverpool Bay. Since 2006 she has been used as a cafe, bar and museum in Canning Dock.

[46] Diomed – Built in 1956 – DWT: 7,980 – In 1970 she was transferred to Glen Line and renamed Glenbeg. In 1972 she reverted to Diomed and in 1973 was sold to Macao and renamed Kaising.

[47] Atreus – Built in 1951 – DWT: 7,800 – In 1977 she was sold to Sherwood Shipping Company, Singapore and renamed United Valiant.

[48] Memnon – Built in 1959 – DWT: 8,504 – In 1975 she was renamed Stentor and in 1977 transferred to Elder Dempster Line and renamed Owerri. In 1978 she was sold to Greece and renamed Europe.

[49] Glenartney – Built in 1940 – DWT: 9,795 – Scrapped in 1967.

[50] Rhexenor – Built in 1945 – DWT: 10,199 – Scrapped in 1975.

[51] Gorgon – Built in 1933 – DWT: 3,533 – A joint Blue Funnel and West Australia company, she was scrapped in 1964.

[52] Breckonshire – Built in 1940 – DWT: 9,061 – In 1941 requisitioned and renamed Empire Activity. In 1942 she became HMS Activity. In 1946 she was returned to Glen Line and renamed Breckonshire. Scrapped in 1967.

[53] Despite our best efforts, unfortunately, we were unable to find the history of this vessel in the correct time period or at least any information that was available to research online.

[54] Despite our best efforts, unfortunately, we were unable to find the history of this vessel in the correct time period or at least any information that was available to research online.

[55] Hector – Built in 1949 – DWT: 10,125 – Scrapped in 1972.

[56] Jason – Built in 1950 – DWT: 10,125 – Scrapped in 1972.

[57] Canberra – Launched in 1960 – Operated originally under the

combined P&O–Orient Line service between the United Kingdom and Australasia. After service in the Falklands war [1982], she continued as a cruise liner under various owners and operators until her last voyage in October 1997 and sold for scrap.

[58] Orcades – Built in 1948 – DWT: 28,472 – Originally built for the Orient Line, in 1962 transferred to P&O Line ownership and in 1973 she was scrapped.

[59] Helenus – Built in 1949 – DWT: 10,125 – Scrapped in 1978.

[60] Tjiwangi – Built in 1950 – DWT: 6,264 – Originally owned and operated by Royal Interocean Lines, she was sold to Pacific International Lines in 1971 and renamed Kota Bali. She was scrapped in 1980.

[61] Arcadia – Launched in 1953 – Owned and operated by P&O. During the 1960's she did a mixture of line voyage interspersed with cruises from Britain and Australia, including trans-Pacific routes. She was scrapped in 1979.

[62] Ellinis – Launched in 1932 – Originally owned by Matson Lines, she was bought by Chandris Lines in 1963 and ran a regular service between England, Greece and Australia. She was scrapped in 1987.

[63] English Star – Built in 1950 – DWT: 9,996 – Owned by Blue Star Line Ltd and she was sold to Chin Tai Enterprise Co. Ltd., Taiwan in 1973 and scrapped.

[64] Eumaeus – Built in 1953 – DWT: 7,681 – In 1962 she was transferred to NSMO (Dutch) and in 1978 scrapped.

ACKNOWLEDGEMENT

We would like to thank several people who supported us during the writing of this book, first and foremost being Cathy and Linda who's love and support was never ending and who both agreed this would be something interesting to do, ultimately historical and more importantly would keep us out of trouble for a while and encouraged us both to complete this book when we were gripped with massive procrastination (drinking wine) during the writing, editing and discussions phases on the book.

David, my kind-hearted brother, who encouraged me to go to sea and who, as a navigating apprentice with BP Tankers, was an inspiration then and, more importantly, his continued support as a brother over the last 79 years.

To Captain David Bowley, who magically provided the impetus to finish this bloody thing. Who provided a metric tonne research and photos of the ships I served on and my life at sea. Sometime in August/September 2023 myself and James were discussing the progress of the book, or lack thereof and that we really should get on with it. Then, as if the gods themselves wanted to send a sign, this box of information arrived on my doorstep from your good self and we knew we had to set a date for publication and just crack on with it.

Peter Wallace, who helped make my apprenticeship more bearable by our many meetings in various ports round the globe during our halfdeck days, including our koala adventure during the winter of 1964. We ended up as roommates in Plymouth studying and ultimately he became a godfather to James.

To Zöe for her continued support and love and Victoria for

doing the cover art and dealing with us not being able to make up our minds.

Oskar, who took on the role of taxi driver in chief for James, allowed us to meet each week and 'work on the book', which is now a euphemism for "drinking wine and doing anything but working on the book" similar to "shopping" that you have seen throughout the previous chapters – thank you without your driving services this book would not have seen the light of day.

To the London Nautical School and Captain Harvey in particular, who gave me the encouragement and opportunities to apply for more maritime companies and which ultimately led to my apprenticeship with Blue Funnel.

And finally to all the other people I had the pleasure to sail with during my career at sea, all of whom made it so enjoyable.

BOOKS BY THIS AUTHOR

Ascot To Argelès

James and Linda have been driving to the South of France for the last 15 years with their children and have learnt a great many things and surprised themselves on any number of occasions.

From travelling through the night to avoid the traffic of black weekends to being stuck in traffic outside Rouen on a black weekend because of a complete planning SNAFU.

Their love of the French and country of France has not diminished in all the years of driving 850 miles with kids – find out why by reading Ascot to Argelès.

Dinosaurs, Elves And Imps: A Short Story Collection

Dinosaurs eating the garden, Elves causing mischief, wonderfully wet camping adventures and other short stories to make you giggle. This is a great book for young readers to read themselves or for you to read to them at bedtime! Fun for all the family in one tiny book.

With a bonus camping recipe (no camping required) as tested on hundreds of scouts, guaranteed to make you toot!

Printed in Great Britain
by Amazon

33031697R00131